OS Utilities

OS Utilities

Doug Lowe

Mike Murach & Associates, Inc.

4697 West Jacquelyn Avenue
Fresno, California 93722
(209) 275-3335

Books for OS shops

MVS JCL
MVS TSO
MVS Assembler Language
OS Utilities
OS Debugging for the COBOL Programmer

Development Team

Technical editor: Steve Eckols
Copy editor: Judy Taylor
Book designer: Michael Rogondino
Production director: Steve Ehlers

Library of Congress Catalog Card Number: 80-84103

ISBN 0-911625-11-9

Contents

Preface

If you've ever written a COBOL program to load an ISAM file from
sequential input and wished for an easier way to do it, this book is
for you. If you've ever had to ask a systems programmer to list a
VTOC for you and wished you could do it yourself, this book is for
you. If you've ever tried to update a member of a source library and
ended up with more mistakes than you started with, this book is for
you. In short, this book is for anyone who wants to make his or her
job easier by using the OS utility programs more effectively.

What this book does

This book will show you how to use OS utility programs for the kinds
of applications that occur every day in an OS shop. You'll learn how
to reformat data sets, how to generate large volumes of test data with
just a few control statements, and how to scratch, rename, or create
new data sets. You'll learn how to use the sort/merge utility. You'll
learn the proper way to make backup copies of sequential, ISAM, and
partitioned data sets. And much more.

    And you'll save time. Most programmers spend more time than
they should doing unimportant jobs. With this book, you'll be able to
code utility jobs in a fraction of the time it took before. As a result,
you'll be a more productive programmer. For example, suppose you
need to make a formatted listing of a sequential file. To code and test
a COBOL program for this purpose would probably take an entire
morning. In contrast, you could code an IEBPTPCH utility job in about
15 minutes. Isn't there something more important you could do the
rest of the morning?

    To fully appreciate the value of this book, you should be aware of
how most programmers learn about OS utilities. Typically, a new
programmer (or an old one converting to OS for the first time) picks
up bits and pieces of the OS utilities in a very inefficient way. He
usually begins with the IBM utilities manual, which probably leaves
him more confused than he was before he started. He might consult a
JCL book, but that probably won't help either. Finally, he asks the

resident utilities expert (the one who graduated from MIT with honors) for help. Usually, the expert decides it would be easier to code the job himself, so the trainee is back where he started: he still knows nothing about OS utilities.

Who this book is for

This book is designed for applications programmers—both new and experienced—who need to use OS utility programs. For a new programmer, it can be used as a textbook in a classroom situation or on an individual basis. As a textbook, it is far superior to the IBM utilities manual or any JCL book. For the experienced programmer, this book can replace the IBM manual as a desk reference. (Since there may be occasional need for the IBM manual, I recommend that you don't throw it away. But feel free to let it gather dust in a dark closet, because with this book on your desk you won't be using that IBM manual very often.)

There is one prerequisite for this book: You should know at least a basic subset of OS JCL. For the experienced programmer, this requirement should present no problems. For a new programmer, this requirement is best met by a formal training program. Fortunately, this book works well with such programs. In fact, *OS Utilities* is a companion to my *MVS JCL* book. Since *OS Utilities* requires only chapters 1-5 of *MVS JCL* as background, students can learn to use the utilities early in their careers.

Some features of this book

Content selection   In deciding what utilities to cover in this book, I've tried to focus on the utility functions that are likely to be required by an applications programmer. As a result, this book covers the utilities used to create, copy, print, and update various types of data sets, to list important system information such as catalog entries or VTOC entries, to sort files, and to process VSAM files. On the other hand, utilities that aren't commonly used by applications programmers aren't covered in this book. Thus, you won't find utilities to initialize disk or tape volumes, to retrieve data from a defective disk track, or to replace TTR entries in the supervisor call library.

Illustrations   We know from experience that a complex subject like OS utilities cannot be learned without extensive illustrative material. In fact, I believe the illustrative material is more important than the descriptive material. That's why this book contains well over a hundred illustrations, including dozens of typical job streams. To illustrate the deficiencies of most training materials when it comes to illustrative material, consider the IBM utilities manual. For the IEBPTPCH (print-punch) utility, the IBM manual provides nine examples, most of them irrelevant. It provides an example of printing a file from a 9-track tape, another example for a 7-track tape, one for a 3330 disk device, an example for a 2314 disk, and one for a 2311 disk, even though these different input devices have no effect on the coding required to execute the utility, other than the VOL and UNIT parameters in the DD statement defining the input file. One of the examples specifies that the control statements are stored as a library member, but doesn't include a listing of the control statements in the member. And with all of this, the IBM manual fails to provide a single example of a simple unformatted print operation! In contrast, chapter 3 of this book, which covers the IEBPTPCH utility, provides a series of simple yet relevant examples that show how to print sequential files with various types of formatting.

Organization   This book is organized in a way that allows you to study the individual utilities in any sequence you want. The only restriction is that you read chapter 1 first. After that, feel free to skip to any chapter you wish.

If you are using this book as a desk reference, this is important to you because it allows you to learn how to use a given utility as the need arises. For example, if you need to use the IEBCOPY utility, you can turn immediately to chapter 5 and learn how.

If you are in charge of training for your company, or if you're an instructor at a college, this organization allows you to design a course around your own requirements and resources. For example, you could spend one one-hour session on each chapter, or cover several utilities in a longer session. And you can decide which utilities you wish to cover and which ones you wish to omit.

Conclusion

As far as I know, this book is the first of its kind. No other book on the market today is devoted to teaching the OS utilities the way they are used every day by applications programmers. And no other book that I know of is able to replace the IBM utilities manual for most applications the way this book can.

Although I believe this book is the most effective training material available for OS utilities, I welcome your comments, criticisms, suggestions, and questions. If you have any, please use the postage-paid comment form near the end of this book. With the help of your comments, I hope we can improve not only this product, but future products as well.

Doug Lowe
Fresno, California
November, 1980

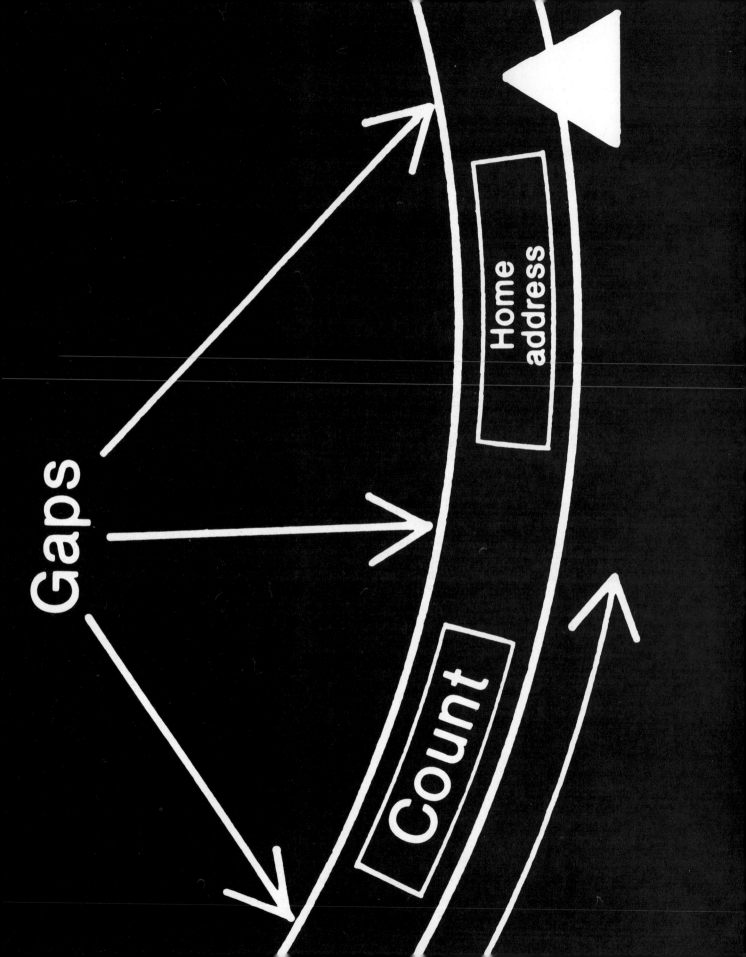

1

An Introduction to OS Utility Programs

A *utility program* (or just *utility*) is a generalized program that can be used for common data processing functions. For example, computer installations frequently copy sequential files. To write a separate program to copy each file would be a waste of programming effort. So, a utility program is available that can copy any sequential file. Similarly, utilities are available to print files, to copy ISAM files, and to update partitioned data sets. The average programmer could write a program to accomplish any one of these functions, but, to save programming effort, utility programs are supplied.

This book shows you how to use most of the utilities IBM supplies with its full Operating System (OS). In this chapter, I'll show you what utilities are available, what they do, and how to choose the right one for a specific application. Then, I'll show you the basics of using the utilities—how to set up the JCL and how to code the control statements.

THE OS UTILITY PROGRAMS

IBM supplies many different utility programs with OS. Figure 1-1 lists those I'm going to cover in this book. These are the utility programs that are most often used by programmers. Here's a description of each:

IEBGENER IEBGENER is the most commonly used IBM utility. Its primary purpose is to make copies of sequential files, but it is often used

Program name	Function
IEBGENER	Makes copies of sequential data sets.
IEBPTPCH	Prints or punches sequential or partitioned data sets.
IEBISAM	Prints, copies, or unloads ISAM data sets.
IEBCOPY	Makes copies of partitioned data sets.
IEBUPDTE	Updates members of partitioned data sets.
IEBDG	Generates test data sets—sequential or ISAM.
IEBCOMPR	Compares sequential or partitioned data sets.
IEHLIST	Lists system data (catalogs, VTOCs, PDS directories).
IEHMOVE	Copies data sets.
IEHPROGM	Catalogs, uncatalogs, scratches, or renames data sets.
IEFBR14	Catalogs, uncatalogs, scratches, or creates null data sets.
Sort/Merge	Sorts or merges sequential data sets.
IDCAMS	VSAM general-purpose utility program.

Figure 1-1 OS utility programs covered in this book

to print sequential files or create partitioned data sets. It is covered in chapter 2.

IEBPTPCH   IEBPTPCH is used to print or punch sequential or partitioned files. It is covered in chapter 3.

IEBISAM   IEBISAM is used to copy, print, or unload ISAM files. For any application involving ISAM files, IEBISAM is a vital utility program. It is covered in chapter 4.

IEBCOPY   IEBCOPY is used to copy partitioned data sets. It is often used to create backup copies of important libraries, merge several libraries together, or compress a library file that contains unused space. It is covered in chapter 5.

IEBUPDTE   IEBUPDTE is IBM's library update utility. It is used primarily to make changes in source libraries. Many shops use a library maintenance system such as PANVALET or LIBRARIAN instead of the IBM utility. But if your shop doesn't have one of these packages, IEBUPDTE can be used. It is covered in chapter 6.

IEBDG   IEBDG is a test-data generator that is used to simplify program testing. IEBDG can also be used to create an ISAM file from sequential input (IEBISAM can't). It is covered in chapter 7.

IEBCOMPR   IEBCOMPR is used to compare two sequential or partitioned files. IEBCOMPR simply reads the two files and determines if they are identical. It is covered in chapter 8.

IEHLIST   IEHLIST has three functions: (1) to list the directory of a partitioned data set, (2) to list entries in a Volume Table of Contents, and (3) to list catalog entries. It is covered in chapter 9.

IEHMOVE   IEHMOVE duplicates the functions of IEBGENER and IEBCOPY: it creates copies of sequential or partitioned files. It is covered in chapter 10. As you will see when you read that chapter, there are several advantages to using IEHMOVE instead of IEBGENER or IEBCOPY.

IEHPROGM   IEHPROGM is used to catalog, uncatalog, scratch, or rename data sets. It is covered in chapter 11.

IEFBR14   IEFBR14 is a ''do nothing'' program that allows you to process file dispositions through the JCL. Thus, with IEFBR14 you can catalog, uncatalog, scratch, or create null data sets. It is covered in chapter 12.

Sort/Merge   The IBM sort/merge program can sort or merge the records of standard sequential files. It is covered in chapter 13.

IDCAMS   IDCAMS is a special utility program available only on VS systems. IDCAMS does for VSAM files what IEBGENER, IEBPTPCH, IEBISAM, IEHLIST, and IEHPROGM do for non-VSAM files. In addition, IDCAMS can perform many of its functions on non-VSAM files. It is covered in chapter 14.

Selecting the right utility

To select the right utility for any given function, you may consult figure 1-1 and the preceding discussion. Or, you may use the table in appendix A. This table presents the utilities by function rather than by program name. Once you have located the correct function in the left-hand column, the column in the middle tells you which utilities may be used. For example, if you look up ''copy sequential files,'' you will see that two utilities may be used: IEBGENER or IEHMOVE. Then, you can select the one you feel more comfortable with. The right-hand

column in appendix A tells you the page number of the chapter that
covers that utility.

Of course, as you become more and more familiar with the utility
programs, you will need this table less and less. But until you feel
comfortable with the utilities, consult this table as often as necessary.

USING THE UTILITY PROGRAMS

The IBM utility programs are executed just like any other program.
Thus, you must be able to code the required job-control statements. In
addition, nearly all of the utility programs require *control cards* (or
control statements) to tell them exactly how to perform their
functions.

JCL requirements

The JCL required to execute utility programs follows one general
pattern with minor variations. In the chapters that follow, I'll show
you these variations. For now, look at the general form in figure 1-2
so you can get an idea of the JCL needed.

The EXEC statement identifies the utility program by name. (The
names of the utilities are given in figure 1-1.) A few of the utility
programs use the PARM parameter to set a mode of execution or to
specify additional information, such as the number of lines to print on
a page. For example, PARM = NEW means that a new data set is
being created, while PARM = MOD means that an existing file is to be
modified. Since the utility programs always reside in the system
library, no STEPLIB or JOBLIB DD statement is necessary.

SYSPRINT identifies the output message file. This is the output
normally printed by the utility to let you know how the program ran.
A typical SYSPRINT listing will show the utility control statements,
the input data, and the final result—for example, the new or changed
file. All of the utility programs require SYSPRINT.

SYSUT1 is the name used by many utilities for the main input
file. The DD parameters you must code here are those you would
normally code if you were accessing a file with a program you wrote
yourself—at the minimum, DSN and DISP. If the file isn't cataloged,
more information may be required. Some of the utilities allow you to
use any ddname you wish for the input file (you tell the utility the
ddname in the control statements). Sometimes, the input data will be
supplied in the SYSIN file, described below. In such cases, SYSUT1
can be omitted.

SYSUT2 is the ddname of the output file. Here, you must provide
all the DD parameters necessary to create a new file. If the output

```
//stepname EXEC  PGM=program-name,
//               PARM=parm-value
//SYSPRINT DD    message listing (SYSOUT=A)
//SYSUT1   DD    input file
//SYSUT2   DD    output file
//SYSUT3   DD    work file
//SYSUT4   DD    work file
//SYSIN    DD    control file (usually * or DATA)
         control statements
/*
```

Figure 1-2   General form of the JCL required for utility programs

file already exists and you are changing or extending it, the DISP parameter will be coded OLD or MOD. As with SYSUT1, some of the utilities let you use any ddname you want.

SYSUT3 and SYSUT4 are used by a few of the utilities for work files. They usually define temporary files on direct-access devices with no DSNAME specified. The DISP parameter is usually coded (NEW,DELETE).

Most of the utility programs require a SYSIN DD statement to identify the file containing the utility control statements. Usually, it is coded DD * to introduce control statements in the input stream. If JCL statements are required in the control file, DD DATA may be coded. Alternatively, you can put the control statements in a library. In this case, instead of an asterisk or the word DATA, the DD statement gives the DSNAME and other attributes of the file containing the control statements.

Control statements

Utility control statements (or cards) are used to tell the utility exactly what you want it to do. To code control statements, you must follow these rules:

1.   Utility control statements are coded in 80-column card format. Positions 1 through 71 are used for the statement, position 72 may be used for a continuation character, and positions 73 through 80 may be used for optional identification or sequence numbers.

2. All utility control statements follow this general format:

```
label operation operands comments
```

These four fields are used as follows:

   a. The label identifies the statement and, if coded, usually must begin in the first position of the statement. In actual practice, the label field is rarely used.

   b. The operation field specifies the type of control statement. It must be preceded and followed by a space. Thus, if the label field is omitted, the operation field must begin *after* position 1.

   c. The operands field is composed of parameters separated by commas. It should be preceded and followed by at least one space.

   d. The comments field is optional. If you code it, it must be preceded and followed by at least one space.

3. To continue a control statement to another line or card, you must place a non-blank character in position 72 and begin the continued statement in position 16 of the next line.

There are two notable exceptions to these rules. The first is the IEBUPDTE utility. All control statements used by IEBUPDTE must have a period in position 1 and a slash in position 2.
For example,

```
./  ADD NAME=TRANREC
```

is an acceptable IEBUPDTE control statement. The second exception is the IDCAMS program. IDCAMS control statements have a totally different set of coding rules that will be covered in chapter 14.

DISCUSSION

At this point, you have the background needed to learn how to use any of the OS utility programs presented in this book. The remainder of this book is organized independently. Thus, you don't have to read the chapters in any particular order. So if you need to use the IEBUPDTE utility right now, skip ahead to chapter 6 and find out how. Or, if you need to use IDCAMS, read chapter 14 next.

One point you may have begun to notice in this chapter is that although the utilities all have many things in common, there are minor differences between them that tend to cause major problems. For example, some of the utilities use SYSUT1 for an input file, some of them allow you to specify your own name, and one of them,

IEHMOVE, uses the ddname SYSUT1 for a work file. So the generalized JCL pattern presented in this chapter is just that—a generalized pattern.

Terminology

utility program

utility

control card

control statement

Objectives

1. Given a description of a problem involving a common utility function, identify the utility program or programs that may be used for the function.
2. List the JCL statements required by most of the utilities.
3. List the general rules for coding utility control statements.

1 1 1 1 1 1 1 1 1 1 1 1

2 2 2 2 2 2 2 2 2 2 2 2

3 3 3 3 3 3 3 3 3 3 3

4 4 4 4 4 4 4 4 4 4 4

5 5 5 5 5 5 5 5 5 5 5

2

The IEBGENER Utility

IEBGENER is one of the most frequently used utility programs. Its basic purpose is to copy sequential data sets, but optional features allow it to manipulate each record as it is copied. IEBGENER can be used to:

- copy a sequential file
- reorganize records in a sequential file
- change the record or block length of a sequential file
- print the contents of a sequential file

Although the most common use of IEBGENER is for simple copy operations, you may need to use it to reorganize data records or change a file's record or block length. This chapter is designed to show you how to use IEBGENER for simple as well as complex copy operations.

IEBGENER is capable of copying sequential data sets using any type of storage device for input or output. For example, you can create a sequential disk file from card input. Or, you can copy a disk file to tape. You can even print a sequential file by specifying SYSOUT = A for the output file. Thus, the functions of IEBGENER overlap somewhat with the functions of IEBPTPCH. In fact, many programmers use IEBGENER instead of IEBPTPCH to print sequential files because IEBGENER is easier to use.

JCL REQUIREMENTS

The JCL requirements for IEBGENER are illustrated in figure 2-1. IEBGENER requires the usual DD statements mentioned in chapter 1. The message listing file, SYSPRINT, is usually coded SYSOUT = A. SYSUT1 is the input file. If the output file, SYSUT2, is a new disk file, you must remember to specify DISP = NEW and the SPACE parameter. In addition, it's a good idea to code the LRECL, BLKSIZE, and RECFM options for a new file. That way, the physical characteristics of the file are documented when the file is created.

For a standard copy operation, no control statements are required. As a result, you can code the SYSIN DD statement with the DUMMY operand. But remember that IEBGENER always requires a SYSIN DD statement, even though it may not be followed by any control statements. If you omit the SYSIN DD statement, the program will terminate.

CONTROL STATEMENTS

If you want to make any modifications to the input records, such as rearranging fields or altering block or record lengths, you must use control statements. Three control statements are commonly used for IEBGENER: the GENERATE statement, the MEMBER statement, and the RECORD statement. They are illustrated in figure 2-2.

The GENERATE statement

Figure 2-2 shows the format of the GENERATE statement. As you can see, three parameters are shown (there is one other that isn't illustrated here, but it isn't used very often). MAXNAME specifies the number of MEMBER statements in the control file; it is almost always coded 1 when it is used. The MAXFLDS parameter indicates how

```
//stepname EXEC  PGM=IEBGENER
//SYSPRINT DD   message listing (SYSOUT=A)
//SYSUT1   DD   input file
//SYSUT2   DD   output file
//SYSIN    DD   control file (* or DUMMY)
      control statements
/*
```

Figure 2-1 JCL requirements for the IEBGENER utility

The GENERATE statement

```
GENERATE MAXNAME=n,
         MAXFLDS=n,
         MAXLITS=n
```

Explanation

MAXNAME   The number of names specified in MEMBER statements.

MAXFLDS   The number of FIELD parameters in RECORD statements.

MAXLITS   The number of bytes of literal data included in FIELD parameters in RECORD statements.

The MEMBER statement

```
MEMBER NAME=name
```

Explanation

NAME   The name of the member to be created if the output is a partitioned data set.

The RECORD statement

$$\text{RECORD FIELD=(length,} \begin{Bmatrix} \text{in-loc} \\ \text{'literal'} \end{Bmatrix} \text{,conv,out-loc)}$$

Explanation

FIELD   Defines the fields in the output record. You can include as many FIELD parameters in a RECORD statement as you need. The following values may be coded:

    length   Specifies the length of the field in the input record.

    in-loc   Specifies the starting position of the field in the input record.

    literal   Used instead of in-loc to supply a literal value to the output field.

    conv   Specifies how the data is to be converted. Code XE to convert to hexadecimal, PZ to unpack packed fields, ZP to pack unpacked fields, or HE to convert BCD fields to EBCDIC. If omitted, no conversion is done.

    out-loc   Specifies the starting position of the field in the output record.

Figure 2-2   The IEBGENER control statements

many FIELD parameters are coded in RECORD statements in the control file. Finally, MAXLITS is used if literal values are included in RECORD statements.

To illustrate the use of the GENERATE statement, consider this example:

```
GENERATE MAXFLDS=2
```

Here, the MAXFLDS parameter means that there will be a RECORD statement with two FIELD parameters. If you omit the MAXNAME parameter, IEBGENER assumes the output will be a standard sequential file. And since MAXLITS isn't coded, no literals can be used in RECORD statements.

The MEMBER statement

The format of the MEMBER statement is shown in the middle part of figure 2-2. It is only used when the output file is partitioned. Quite simply, it specifies the name of the member that IEBGENER is to create. For example,

```
MEMBER NAME=AR401
```

means to create a library member named AR401. If the MEMBER statement isn't used, IEBGENER produces a standard sequential file as output.

The RECORD statement

The RECORD statement, illustrated in the bottom part of figure 2-2, is used to specify formatting and conversion instructions for various fields in the input record. One FIELD parameter is coded for each field to be included in the output record. Each FIELD parameter specifies the field's length, its location in the input record, what type of conversion should be done on the field, and where it should be placed in the output record.

As a simple illustration, suppose you are copying a file whose records contain three fields:

Column	Description
1-5	Item number
6-10	Quantity on hand
11-15	Unit price

As you copy the file, you want to rearrange the order of these fields so the output file has this format:

Column	Description
1-5	Unit price
6-10	Item number
11-15	Quantity on hand

To do this, you code a RECORD statement with three FIELD parameters, like this:

```
RECORD FIELD=(5,1,,6),FIELD=(5,6,,11),
       FIELD=(5,11,,1)
```

Here, the first FIELD parameter says to move the five bytes starting at position 1 in the input record to the five bytes starting at position 6 in the output record. Similarly, the next two FIELD parameters move the data from its original position in the input record to its new position in the output record.

Notice how two commas were coded in a row in each of the FIELD parameters in the last example. That's because the conversion specification was omitted. If you wish to convert the data in a field from one form to another, you can specify one of these values:

Value	Meaning
PZ	Convert from packed to unpacked (zoned)
ZP	Convert from unpacked (zoned) to packed
HE	Convert from BCD to EBCDIC
XE	Convert to hexadecimal notation

For example, consider this RECORD statement:

```
RECORD FIELD=(3,1,PZ,1),FIELD=(5,4,,6)
```

Here, the data in the first three bytes of the input record is unpacked and moved to the output record. Then, the data in bytes 4-8 of the input record is moved to bytes 6-10 of the output record. When the three bytes of packed data are unpacked, they take up five bytes in the output record. Thus, the second field starts in position 6 instead of position 4.

Instead of a number indicating a field's input location, you can code a FIELD parameter with a literal value. To illustrate, consider this RECORD statement:

```
RECORD FIELD=(5,'ABCDE',,1)
```

Here, the literal value ABCDE is placed in bytes 1-5 of the output record. Notice that when a literal is specified, the length value must still be coded and the literal itself must be coded between single quotation marks.

When you use a literal in this way, the MAXLITS parameter of the GENERATE statement must be coded. MAXLITS indicates the total number of bytes of literal data included in FIELD parameters. So, if you only included one literal whose length was five bytes, you would code MAXLITS = 5.

Suppose, however, that you include several literals, as in this RECORD statement:

```
RECORD FIELD=(5,'ABCDE',,1),
       FIELD=(4,'****',,10),
       FIELD=(3,'123',,15)
```

When you have more than one literal, you add the lengths of all the literals together to get the value to code on the MAXLITS parameter. In this case, you would code MAXLITS = 12, because the lengths of the literals are five, four, and three.

IEBGENER EXAMPLES

Now that you have seen the JCL and control statements for IEBGENER, I want to show you a few examples of this utility's use. The first three examples show basic IEBGENER setups for copying sequential files using various devices for input and output. The fourth example shows a copy operation that creates a partitioned data set. The fifth example shows a copy operation with simple editing.

Example 1: Creating a sequential file from card input

Figure 2-3 shows an IEBGENER job that copies a deck of cards to a sequential disk file. As you can see, no control statements are used, so the input records are copied directly into the output file. SYSUT2 defines the output file with the name H4.ITCRDS, and SYSUT1 defines the input card file. Since SYSUT2 is a new data set, the SPACE parameter is coded, as is the DCB parameter with the RECFM, LRECL, and BLKSIZE options.

Example 2: Copying a sequential file

Figure 2-4 shows the JCL requirements for making a copy of a sequential file. Again, no control statements are used, so the utility assumes that this is a standard copy operation. The SYSUT1 DD statement defines the input file (H4.INVTRAN), a cataloged data set. The SYSUT2 DD statement defines the output file with the same DSNAME, but directs it to a volume named OSTR36. Although it isn't required, I always code a DCB parameter for the output file.

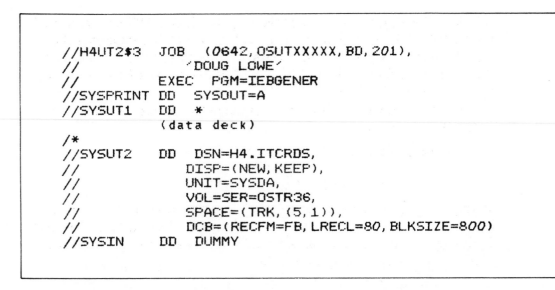

```
//H4UT2$3   JOB   (0642,OSUTXXXXX,BD,201),
//                'DOUG LOWE'
//          EXEC  PGM=IEBGENER
//SYSPRINT DD   SYSOUT=A
//SYSUT1    DD   *
           (data deck)
/*
//SYSUT2    DD   DSN=H4.ITCRDS,
//               DISP=(NEW,KEEP),
//               UNIT=SYSDA,
//               VOL=SER=OSTR36,
//               SPACE=(TRK,(5,1)),
//               DCB=(RECFM=FB,LRECL=80,BLKSIZE=800)
//SYSIN     DD   DUMMY
```

Figure 2-3   Creating a sequential disk file from card input using IEBGENER

```
//H4UT2$4   JOB   (0642,OSUTXXXXX,BD,201),
//                'DOUG LOWE'
//          EXEC  PGM=IEBGENER
//SYSPRINT DD   SYSOUT=A
//SYSUT1    DD   DSN=H4.INVTRAN,
//               DISP=OLD
//SYSUT2    DD   DSN=H4.INVTRAN,
//               DISP=(NEW,KEEP),
//               UNIT=SYSDA,
//               VOL=SER=OSTR36,
//               SPACE=(TRK,(10,10)),
//               DCB=(RECFM=FB,LRECL=100,BLKSIZE=1000)
//SYSIN     DD   DUMMY
```

Figure 2-4   Copying a sequential file using IEBGENER

Example 3: Printing a member of a partitioned data set

Figure 2-5 shows how IEBGENER can be used to print the contents of a member of a partitioned data set. Here, SYSUT1 specifies the library (H4.COB.COPYLIB) and the member name (BFREC). SYSUT2 specifies that the output is to be directed to the printer (SYSOUT = A).

```
//H4UTZ$5   JOB   (0642,OSUTXXXXX,BD,201),
//               'DOUG LOWE'
//          EXEC  PGM=IEBGENER
//SYSPRINT DD   SYSOUT=A
//SYSUT1    DD   DSN=H4.COB.COPYLIB(BFREC),
//               DISP=SHR
//SYSUT2    DD   SYSOUT=A
//SYSIN     DD   DUMMY
```

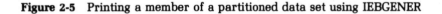

Figure 2-5   Printing a member of a partitioned data set using IEBGENER

Again, since no control statements are used, IEBGENER simply copies each input record directly to the printer. If the input records are longer than 132 positions, however, they will be truncated when printed.

Example 4: Creating a library member

Figure 2-6 shows an IEBGENER job to create a member in a partitioned data set. Since the library file already exists, SYSUT2 is coded with DISP = OLD and no SPACE operand. And since the output is partitioned, control statements are required. The first one, the GENERATE statement, simply indicates that one MEMBER statement will follow by specifying MAXNAME = 1. Then, the MEMBER statement identifies the name of the new member as INVREC. No RECORD statement is included, so the SYSUT1 file is copied directly into the library file.

Example 5: Copying a sequential file with editing

To illustrate the use of IEBGENER's editing capabilities, consider the problem of switching from a five-digit zip code to a nine-digit zip code. (This is a problem we are all going to encounter in the 1980s.) A file can be modified to accommodate this change in two ways. First, an extra four bytes can be added to the zip code field, bringing its length to nine bytes. The alternative is to pack the zip code field, allowing for nine digits. (Of course, this method won't work if the zip code is already packed.)

Suppose, for example, that it's necessary to convert the format of an accounts receivable master file as shown in figure 2-7 to accommodate the expanded zip code. Figure 2-8 shows an IEBGENER job for converting the file, named H4.ARMAST, using the first method. As you can see in figure 2-7, the zip code in the input record is stored in

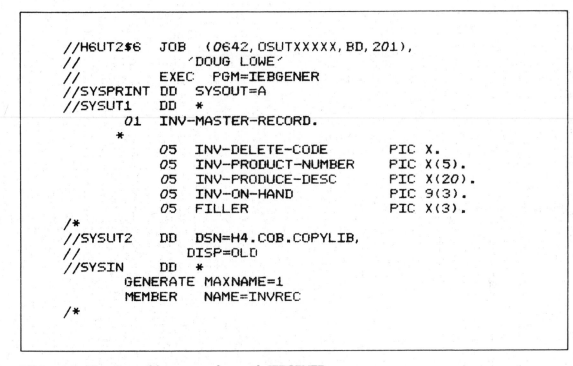

```
//H6UTZ$6   JOB   (0642,OSUTXXXXX,BD,201),
//                'DOUG LOWE'
//          EXEC  PGM=IEBGENER
//SYSPRINT  DD    SYSOUT=A
//SYSUT1    DD    *
     01   INV-MASTER-RECORD.
        *
          05   INV-DELETE-CODE      PIC X.
          05   INV-PRODUCT-NUMBER   PIC X(5).
          05   INV-PRODUCE-DESC     PIC X(20).
          05   INV-ON-HAND          PIC 9(3).
          05   FILLER               PIC X(3).
/*
//SYSUT2    DD    DSN=H4.COB.COPYLIB,
//                DISP=OLD
//SYSIN     DD    *
      GENERATE MAXNAME=1
      MEMBER   NAME=INVREC
/*
```

Figure 2-6 Creating a library member with IEBGENER

positions 96-100. In the output record, the zip code will be expanded
to occupy positions 96-104. Thus the length of the record will be
increased from 116 bytes to 120 bytes. This change in record length
is reflected in the DCB parameter for SYSUT2.

The control statements for this job look like this:

```
GENERATE MAXFLDS=3,MAXLITS=4
RECORD   FIELD=(100,1,,1),
         FIELD=(4,'0000',,101),
         FIELD=(16,101,,105)
```

The first FIELD parameter says to move the first 100 bytes of the
input record to the output record as is. Then, the next FIELD
parameter moves a literal value of 0000 into bytes 101-104, thus
adding four bytes to the zip code. Then, the last FIELD parameter
moves the remainder of the input record to the output record, offset
by four bytes.

DISCUSSION

In general, the IEBGENER program has two uses. The first is for
routine file copying, especially for backup or print operations. For
this usage, IEBGENER is used with no control statements. The second

Old record format

Field Name	Cust. No.	Salesman No.	Cust. Name	Cust. Address-1	Cust. Address-2	Cust. City	Cust. State	Cust. Zip Code	Cust. Credit Limit	Cust. Balance Due
Characteristics										
Position	1-6	7-12	13-34	35-56	57-78	79-93	94-95	96-100	101-108	109-116

New record format

Field Name	Cust. No.	Salesman No.	Cust. Name	Cust. Address-1	Cust. Address-2	Cust. City	Cust. State	Cust. Zip Code	Cust. Credit Limit	Cust. Balance Due
Characteristics										
Position	1-6	7-12	13-34	35-56	57-78	79-93	94-95	96-104	105-112	113-120

Figure 2-7 Original accounts receivable master file with a five-digit zip code (top) and modified accounts receivable master file with a nine-digit zip code (bottom)

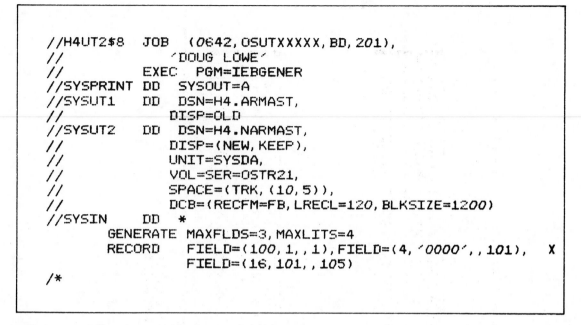

```
//H4UT2$8    JOB   (0642,OSUTXXXXX,BD,201),
//                 'DOUG LOWE'
//           EXEC  PGM=IEBGENER
//SYSPRINT DD   SYSOUT=A
//SYSUT1    DD   DSN=H4.ARMAST,
//               DISP=OLD
//SYSUT2    DD   DSN=H4.NARMAST,
//               DISP=(NEW,KEEP),
//               UNIT=SYSDA,
//               VOL=SER=OSTR21,
//               SPACE=(TRK,(10,5)),
//               DCB=(RECFM=FB,LRECL=120,BLKSIZE=1200)
//SYSIN     DD   *
          GENERATE MAXFLDS=3,MAXLITS=4
          RECORD    FIELD=(100,1,,1),FIELD=(4,'0000',,101),    X
                    FIELD=(16,101,,105)
/*
```

Figure 2-8   Editing a sequential file with IEBGENER

use is for occasional system modifications, such as the zip-code
expansion just described. Other examples of this type of application
are converting a card file to a tape file where numeric data can be
packed, converting a sequential file to an ISAM file where a delete
code needs to be added in the first byte of each record, or converting
an ISAM file to a VSAM file, where the delete byte needs to be
removed. For these uses, the IEBGENER control statements are
normally required. (Remember that IEBGENER can't actually create
an ISAM or a VSAM file. But it can create a sequential file in the
proper format, which can then be converted into an ISAM file using
the IEBDG utility, or into a VSAM file using the IDCAMS utility.)

Objective

Given the requirements of a file-copy operation, code an acceptable
IEBGENER job. If changes to the records are required, code
appropriate control statements.

```
      (0642.DMTEST1XX
'DOUG LOWE'
C   PGM=IEFBR14
 DUMMY
 DSN=H4.CAPPRL.
DISP=(NEW.CATLG).
UNIT=SYSDA.
VOL=SER=OSTR47.
SPACE=(TRK.(10.2)
DCB(LRECL=90.BLKS
C   PGM=IEFBR14
 DSN=H4.CAPPRL.
DISP=OLD
 SYSOUT=A
```

3

The IEBPTPCH Utility

One of the most commonly used utility programs is IEBPTPCH, often called the print-punch utility. IEBPTPCH can be used to:

• print a sequential file or a member of a partitioned data set

• punch a sequential file or a member of a partitioned data set

• format the printed or punched output

Although IEBPTPCH can be used to produce either printed or punched output, it is normally used for print operations.

The print-punch utility is often used when testing programs. For example, suppose you are testing a program that updates a master file of inventory records. You can use the IEBPTPCH utility to list the contents of the master file before and after it has been updated. Then, you can check the listings to be sure the file was updated properly.

The print-punch utility also has the capability of formatting the data to make the output more readable. For example, suppose the inventory master file you were updating contained fifteen data fields. IEBPTPCH allows you to space these fields out on the listing so they are easy to read. In addition, if some of the fields are packed-decimal, IEBPTPCH can unpack them. Or, alternatively, you can specify that they be converted to hexadecimal format. In short, IEBPTPCH provides considerable control over the format of the listing.

JCL REQUIREMENTS

Figure 3-1 shows the JCL statements needed to execute the print-punch utility. As you can see, IEBPTPCH requires four files. The first one, SYSPRINT, is the message file. It should be treated as normal printed output (SYSOUT = A). The second file, SYSUT1, is the input file. This is the file that is to be listed by IEBPTPCH. The third file is SYSUT2; it describes the output file, usually specified as SYSOUT = A. The fourth file, SYSIN, is the file containing the control statements. The control statements are usually coded as instream data (DD *), but sometimes SYSIN will refer to a library member.

CONTROL STATEMENTS

Like the other utility programs, IEBPTPCH requires control statements that specify how it is to execute. You may supply several control statements to IEBPTPCH. The most frequently used ones are PRINT, PUNCH, TITLE, RECORD, and MEMBER. They are described below.

The PRINT statement

The PRINT statement is the primary control statement for the print-punch utility. For printing operations, it must be the first statement in the control file. In its simplest form, it is coded like this:

```
PRINT
```

Here, no parameters are coded. When the PRINT statement is used in this way, the input data is printed in groups of eight characters with each group separated by two blanks. The utility can print up to 112 characters (12 groups of eight) on one line. If the input record contains more than 112 characters, it is continued on the next line.

Figure 3-2 shows the complete format of the PRINT statement. As you can see, many parameters may be coded on the PRINT statement.

```
//stepname EXEC  PGM=IEBPTPCH
//SYSPRINT DD   message listing (SYSOUT=A)
//SYSUT1   DD   input file
//SYSUT2   DD   output file (usually SYSOUT=A)
//SYSIN    DD   control file (usually *)
     control statements
/*
```

Figure 3-1   JCL requirements for the IEBPTPCH utility

```
The PRINT statement

PRINT  PREFORM= {A}
                {M} ,

       TYPORG= {PS}
               {PO} ,

       TOTCONV= {XE}
                {PZ} ,

       CNTRL=n,

       STRTAFT=n,

       STOPAFT=n,

       SKIP=n,

       MAXNAME=n,

       MAXFLDS=n,

       INITPG=n,

       MAXLINE=n
```

Figure 3-2   The PRINT statement (part 1 of 2)

But none of them are difficult to understand, and you will probably
only use a few of them.

The TOTCONV parameter is used when you want to convert the
input data from one format to another. There are two types of
conversion IEBPTPCH can do. The first is conversion of data to
hexadecimal notation. When this type of conversion is used, the data
will print two characters per byte, much like a storage dump. To
specify hexadecimal conversion, code TOTCONV = XE. The second
type of conversion is from packed decimal to zoned decimal. This is
specified by coding TOTCONV = PZ. When the TOTCONV operand is
coded, the entire input record is converted as specified. If you wish to
convert only certain fields in the record, you must specify the FIELD
operand in the RECORD statement (I'll show you how in a minute).

The STRTAFT, STOPAFT, and SKIP parameters are used to
indicate that only a portion of the input file is to be listed. For
example, consider this PRINT statement:

```
PRINT  STRTAFT=100
```

This indicates that IEBPTPCH should skip the first 100 records in the
input file before printing. Similarly,

```
PRINT  STOPAFT=300
```

means that IEBPTPCH should stop after 300 records have been
printed. SKIP is used to indicate that only certain records are to be

Explanation

PREFORM   Specifies that the input file already contains carriage-control
           characters in the first byte of each record. If A is specified, ASA
           characters are assumed; M means machine characters. If you code
           PREFORM, don't code any other parameters on the PRINT
           statement.

TYPORG   Indicates the organization of the input file. PS means sequential; PO
           means partitioned. The default is PS.

TOTCONV   Indicates conversion of the entire input record (as opposed to con-
           version of individual fields specified by the RECORD statement). XE
           means to convert to hexadecimal; PZ means to unpack packed
           decimal fields. If TOTCONV is omitted, no conversion is done.

CNTRL   Specifies the line spacing of the listing. Values can be 1, 2, or 3 for
           single, double, or triple spacing.

STRTAFT   Indicates how many records to skip before printing.

STOPAFT   Specifies the number of records to be printed.

SKIP   Means to print only every nth record. If SKIP is omitted, every
           record is printed.

MAXNAME   Specifies the number of MEMBER statements in the control file.

MAXFLDS   Specifies the number of FIELD parameters in RECORD statements
           in the control file.

INITPG   Specifies the number of the first page. Default is one.

MAXLINE   Specifies the number of lines printed on each page. Default is 60.

Note: The numbers specified for MAXNAME and MAXFLDS can be greater than the required
      numbers but must not be less.

Figure 3-2   The PRINT statement (part 2 of 2)

printed. For example,

```
PRINT SKIP=10
```

indicates that only every tenth record should be printed. These
parameters are used when the input file is large and you don't need
to list all of it.

Two of the PRINT operands (MAXNAME and MAXFLDS) are
used in conjunction with other control statements. MAXNAME
specifies how many MEMBER statements are used, and MAXFLDS
indicates how many FIELD operands are present in RECORD

statements. Although the numbers specified in these parameters don't have to be exact, they must not be less than the correct number. In other words, if you code

```
MAXFLDS=3
```

and then include five FIELD operands, the program will terminate. You will see how these parameters are used later in this chapter.

PRINT statement examples   Figure 3-3 shows some examples of the PRINT statement. In example 1, PRINT is coded with no parameters. As I said before, this causes the utility to print the contents of the input file in a standard format (groups of eight characters separated by two spaces). Example 2 shows how the TOTCONV parameter is used to specify a different format—in this case, the input data is printed in hexadecimal format.

The PRINT statement in example 3 says to print the output listing double spaced, to print every tenth record, and to stop printing after 1000 records have been printed. Finally, example 4 indicates that a RECORD statement will follow having six FIELD parameters.

The PUNCH statement

Figure 3-4 shows the format of the PUNCH statement. The PUNCH statement is intended to be used instead of the PRINT statement when the output is directed to cards (SYSOUT = B). The main differences

---

Example 1

```
PRINT
```

Example 2

```
PRINT TOTCONV=XE
```

Example 3

```
PRINT CNTRL=2,STOPAFT=1000,SKIP=10
```

Example 4

```
PRINT MAXFLDS=6
```

Figure 3-3   Examples of the PRINT statement

The PUNCH statement

PUNCH parms

Explanation

parms	Coded the same as for the PRINT statement, with these exceptions:
PREFORM	Indicates presence of stacker-control characters. A = ASA; M = machine code.
INITPG	Not used for PUNCH statement.
MAXLINE	Not used for PUNCH statement.
CNTRL	Indicates which stacker should be used (1 or 2) rather than output spacing.
CDSEQ	Specifies a starting value for sequence numbers that will be punched in columns 73-80. If CDSEQ is omitted, sequence numbers aren't punched.
CDINCR	Increment for the sequence numbers. Default is ten.

Figure 3-4   The PUNCH statement

between a PRINT and PUNCH operation are: (1) a PUNCH operation allows you to include sequence numbers in the output; and (2) the default format for output from a punch operation causes the data to be punched as a continuous stream, not in groups of eight characters.

Many programmers use the PUNCH statement instead of the PRINT statement to print sequential files because of the way the data is formatted. To do this, you simply use a PUNCH statement instead of a PRINT statement, but still direct the output (SYSUT2) to a printer (SYSOUT = A).

The parameters used by the PUNCH statement are for the most part the same as those used by the PRINT statement, with the differences explained in figure 3-4. Two parameters are unique to the PUNCH statement: CDSEQ and CDINCR. These two parameters are used to punch sequence numbers in the output cards. Although you can't specify in what columns the sequence numbers are to be punched—they always go in columns 73-80—you can specify a starting value using CDSEQ, and an increment value with CDINCR. If you don't want sequence numbers to be punched in the cards, simply omit these two parameters.

The TITLE statement

```
TITLE ITEM=('literal',out-loc)
```

Explanation

ITEM   Specifies title information. These values may be coded:

    literal   The title to be printed.

    out-loc   The starting position of the literal in the title record.
           Default is one.

Figure 3-5   The TITLE statement

The TITLE statement

In some cases, you may want to print a title on your listing. If so, you can use the TITLE statement, illustrated in figure 3-5. If the TITLE statement is used, it must immediately follow the PRINT or PUNCH statement.

The TITLE statement simply specifies a literal that is printed at the beginning of the listing. For example, this TITLE statement

```
TITLE ITEM=('LISTING OF TRANSACTION FILE',20)
```

says to print LISTING OF TRANSACTION FILE beginning in column 20.

The MEMBER statement

The MEMBER statement is used when the input file (SYSUT1) is a partitioned data set. The format of the MEMBER statement is given in figure 3-6. To illustrate how it is used, consider this statement:

```
MEMBER NAME=TRANREC
```

Here, only the member named TRANREC will be printed or punched. If the MEMBER statement isn't specified, every member of the partitioned data set will be printed or punched.

If you wish to print or punch more than one member, you simply code more than one MEMBER statement. To illustrate, consider these statements:

The MEMBER statement

MEMBER NAME=name

Explanation

NAME   Specifies the name of the member to be processed.

Figure 3-6   The MEMBER statement

```
PRINT   TYPORG=PO,STOPAFT=10,MAXNAME=3
MEMBER  NAME=TRANREC
MEMBER  NAME=ORDRREC
MEMBER  NAME=ACRCREC
```

Here, three members from the same library are to be printed. The control information specified in the PRINT statement applies to each of the three members. So in this case, the first ten records of TRANREC are printed, then the first ten records of ORDRREC are printed, and finally the first ten records of ACRCREC are printed. Also, notice how the MAXNAME parameter is used in the PRINT statement to indicate how many MEMBER statements are coded.

The RECORD statement

The RECORD statement, illustrated in figure 3-7, is used to specify formatting and conversion instructions for various fields in the input record. For example, suppose you were printing a record that had this format:

Column	Description
1-5	Item number
6-10	Quantity on hand
11-16	Unit price

Suppose the values of these fields were 10114, 00050, and 001995. If you use a PRINT statement with no formatting, the record would print like this:

```
10114000  50001995
```

Then, you would have to decipher the output listing to determine what the values of the fields were.

The RECORD statement

```
RECORD FIELD=(length,in-loc,conv,out-loc)
```

Explanation

FIELD   Specifies how fields in the input record are to be processed and edited. The FIELD parameter can appear more than once in a RECORD statement. The following values can be coded:

length   Specifies the length of the field in the input record.

in-loc   Specifies the starting location of the field in the input record.

conv   Specifies how the data in the field is to be converted. Code XE to convert to hexadecimal, PZ to unpack packed fields. If omitted, no conversion is done.

out-loc   Specifies the position in which the field should begin in the output record.

Figure 3-7 The RECORD statement

Suppose instead that you want the output listing to look like this:

```
10114   00050   001995
```

You can easily achieve this type of formatting by using a RECORD statement that includes FIELD parameters, one for each of the fields in the input record. Each FIELD parameter specifies the length of the field, its starting position in the input record, a conversion instruction, and the position to which you want the field moved in the output record. For example, consider this RECORD statement:

```
RECORD FIELD=(5,1,,1),
       FIELD=(5,6,,8),
       FIELD=(6,11,,15)
```

Here, the five-byte field beginning in position 1 of the input record will be printed starting in the first print position, the five-byte field beginning in position 6 will be printed starting in position 8, and the six-byte field beginning in position 11 will be printed starting in position 15.

Notice that two commas were coded before the last number in each FIELD parameter. That's because no conversion was specified. If conversion of a field is required, XE or PZ is coded there, like this:

```
RECORD FIELD=(4,1,XE,1)
```

Here, hexadecimal conversion will be done. Be sure to remember that when hexadecimal conversion is done, the resulting output takes twice as many positions as the input—so if the field is four bytes long in the input record, allow eight bytes for it in the output line. When converting from packed to zoned decimal, the resulting field is one byte less than twice the size of the input field—so if the field is three bytes long in the input record, allow five bytes for it in the output line.

IEBPTPCH EXAMPLES

Now that you've seen the individual control statements required by IEBPTPCH, I want to show you some sample IEBPTPCH jobs. These should serve as models for most of the IEBPTPCH jobs you'll ever run.

Example 1: Printing a sequential file with no formatting

Figure 3-8 shows a basic IEBPTPCH job—a simple print operation with no formatting. The top part of this figure shows the JCL and control statements used. The input file is a cataloged file of inventory transactions named H4.INVTRAN. As you can see, the PRINT statement is coded with no parameters. The bottom part of the figure shows the output from this job. As you can see, the data is printed in groups of eight characters—the standard format for a PRINT operation. IEBPTPCH prints an asterisk at the end of each record and two asterisks to mark the end of each block.

For many applications, this type of printing operation is acceptable. But in some cases, a record may contain data that isn't printable (for example, packed-decimal or binary numbers). In such cases, you can convert the data to hexadecimal notation by changing the PRINT statement to this:

```
PRINT TOTCONV=XE
```

Figure 3-9 shows the how the inventory transaction file looks when printed in this format. As you can see, the data is still printed in groups of eight characters. However, each of these groups represents only four bytes of data, because two hexadecimal digits are printed for each data byte. Notice that since each record contained more data than could be printed in hexadecimal notation on one line, IEBPTPCH printed two lines for each input record.

Example 2: Printing a sequential file with formatting

Figure 3-10 shows an IEBPTPCH job to print the same inventory transaction file using format control. The PRINT statement has a

The JCL

```
//H4UT3$8   JOB  (0642,OSUTXXXXX,BD,201),
//               'DOUG LOWE',
//         EXEC  PGM=IEBPTPCH
//SYSPRINT  DD   SYSOUT=A
//SYSUT1    DD   DSN=H4.INVTRAN,
//               DISP=OLD
//SYSUT2    DD   SYSOUT=A
//SYSIN     DD   *
    PRINT
/*
```

Resulting output

```
                                                          * * * * * * * * * * **** * * * * * * * ** * * * * * ** * * * **

01203102  35000256  40026456  01564000  01564000  00016540  15205610  54000160  1540
01687900  89004040  00065100  00546054  60044000  04564000  10654000  01000546  0001
00564000  49015605  40032498  05684001  98004894  00897000  98700654  45600005  4500
05407894  56000000  00000135  46871510  00015615  41000000  00000000  00000000  0000
16874400  26748002  65002598  20000154  00124007  89001264  00018900  15567000  4898
02211022  00447001  47001560  02580013  50015400  12300546  00123005  48001354  0012
08884002  25111002  58014700  39600145  00256002  56036555  00254005  87005689  0025
02541202  54111001  45002560  03650025  40041200  52300698  00587007  45008560  0965
05877702  54015204  58056203  25698501  47502563  20258741  02589632  02582000  0000
05874410  25025100  00012547  89620014  52102365  89652302  14521458  77400025  4125
48795000  00235545  00124501  25410216  59800222  22014759  60140010  02540010  0200
54777100  10020054  41000356  20000441  02020001  22021100  00210002  20000000  0000
10564000  49015605  40032498  05684001  98004894  00897000  98700654  45600005  4500
05874410  25025100  00012547  89620014  52102365  89652302  14521458  77400025  4125
00564000  49015605  40032498  05684001  98004894  00897000  98700654  45600005  4500
02203202  35000256  40026456  02564000  02564000  00026540  25205620  54002060  2540
05407894  56000000  00000235  46872520  00025625  42000000  00000000  45008560  0000
02542202  54222002  45002560  03650025  40042200  52300698  00587007  45008560  0965
54777200  20020054  41000356  20000441  02020001  22021100  00210002  20000000  0000
02203202  35000256  40026456  02564000  02564000  00026540  15205610  54000160  1540
48795000  00235545  00224502  25420216  59800222  22014759  60140010  02540010  0200
02222022  00447002  47002560  02580013  50015400  12300546  00123005  48001354  0012
05877702  54025204  58056203  25698502  47502563  20258741  02589632  02582000  0000
05407894  56000000  00000235  46872510  00015615  41000000  00000000  00000000  0000
02222022  00447002  47001560  02580013  50015400  12300546  00123005  48001354  0012
05877702  54025204  58056203  25698502  47502563  20258742  02589632  02582000  0000
```

Figure 3-8 Printing a sequential file using IEBPTPCH

```
                                                                    PAGE  0001
F0F1F2F0  F3F1F0F2  F3F5F0F0  F4F0F0F2  F6F4F5F6  F0F1F5F6  F4F0F0F0  F0F0F0F1  F6F5F4F0
F1F5F2F0  F5F6F1F0  F5F4F0F0  F1F5F4F0  40404040  40404040  40404040  F0F0F4F5F6 F4F0F0F0
F0F1F6F8  F7F9F0F0  F8F9F0F0  F0F0F0F6  F5F5F1F0F0 F0F0F5F4  F6F0F0F0F0 F0F0F4F5F6
F1F0F6F5  F4F0F0F0  F0F1F0F0  F4F0F0F3  F2F4F9F8  F0F5F6F8  F4F0F0F0F1 F0F0F0F8F9 F7F0F0F0
F0F0F5F6  F0F6F5F4  F4F5F6F0  F4F5F0F0  F4F9F8    F0F1F3F5  F4F0F0F1  F4F8F9F4  F0F0F0F0
F9F8F7F0  F6F5F4    F5F6F0F0  F0F0F0F0  40404040  F4F6F8F7  40404040* F5F6F1F5  F1F2F6F4
F9F8F4F0  F4F4F0F0  F0F0F0F0  F8F0F0F0  F2F5F9F8  40404040  40404040* F4F0F0F7  F0F5F4F6
F0F5F4F0  F8F9F0F0  F1F5F5F6  F7F0F0F0  40404040  F0F0F0F0  F0F1F5F4  F5F4F0F0  F6F5F5F5
F1F6F8F7  F1F0F2F2  F0F0F4F4  F7F0F0F1  F1F5F5F6F0 F0F2F5F8  F0F0F1F3  F6F0F0F2  F0F6F9F8
F0F0F0F0  F3F0F0F5  F0F0F0F0  F1F3F5F4  F4F7F0F0  40404040* F0F0F0F0  F1F2F3F0  F8F7F4F1
F0F2F2F1  F4F0F0F5  F4F8F0F0  F5F8F0F1  F4F7F0F0  F3F9F8F0  40404040* F2F5F6F5  F2F3F0F2
F0F0F1F2  F2F5F5F6  F8F5F0F0  F5F6F8F9  40404040  F0F1F4F5  F0F2F5    F2F3F6F5  F4F7F5F9
F0F0F1F2  F1F4F5F8  F7F7F4F0  F0F0F0F0  F0F0F0F0  40404040* F4F0F0F4  F8F9F6F5  F0F0F0F0
F0F8F8F8  F5F0F0F0  F0F0F0F0  F2F5F6F0  F0F3F6F5  F8F5F0F1  F4F7F5F0  F2F2F0F1  F1F1F0F0
F0F0F2F5  F0F0F1F0  F2F0F2F5  F2F5F6F9  40404040* F5F2F1F0  F2F3F0F2  F0F0F8F9  F7F0F0F0
F0F0F2F5  F7F7F4F0  F2F5F1F0  F8F9F6F2  40404040** F5F9F8F0  F2F3F0F2  F8F9F6F5  F2F3F0F2
F1F2F5F4  F5F0F0F0  F5F5F4F5  F2F5F4F1  F0F2F1F6  F0F2F4F1  F2F2F2    F0F8F9F4  F7F0F0F0
F0F0F5F8  F6F6F5F0  F5F6F6F0  F2F0F0F0  40404040* F0F0F0F1  F2F2F0F2  F6F5F4F0  F6F5F4F0
F0F5F5F8  F3F2F0F0  F2F5F6F0  F4F4F5F6  F4F0F0F1  F9F8F0F0  F0F8F9    F2F2F0F2  F0F0F0F0
F0F5F8F7  F5F6F2F0  F2F5F6F0  F5F4F4F0  40404040* F5F2F1F0  F8F9F6F5  F0F0F0F2  F6F6F9F8
F2F5F4F0  F0F0F0F0  F0F0F0F0  F0F3F5F6  F2F5F2F0  F5F9F8F0  F2F2F5F6  F4F2F0F0  F1F1F0F0
F5F4F7F7  F0F0F0F0  F0F0F0F2  F2F5F6F0  40404040* F4F0F0F4  F2F2FOF5  F2F2F0F2  F7F0F0F0
F5F4F7F7  F0F0F0F0  F2F2F0F2  F0F0F0F0  40404040* F0F2F6F0  F0F0F0F0  F0F0F0F2  F2F3F0F2
F1F5F5F6  F0F0F0F0  F3F5F4F0  F4F5F5F6  F4F0F0F0  F2F5F6F0  F4F0F0F0  F2F5F6F0  F6F5F4F0
F9F8F7F0  F0F0F0F0  F2F5F6F0  F0F0F0F0  F2F5F2F0  F5F9F8F0  F2F2F0F1  F4F4F7F5  F0F0F0F0
F0F0F0F0  F0F0F0F0  F5F6F4F0  F2F5F5F6  40404040* F5F5F0F0  F2F2F0F2  F2F5F5F0  F1F1F0F0
F2F2F5F0  F0F0F0F0  F5F6F6F0  F6F4F5F6  F0F3F6F5  F0F0F0F0  F2F2F5F5  F5F6F1F5  F7F0F0F0
F0F0F0F0  F0F0F0F2  F5F4F2F2  40404040  F0F0F0F0  F4F7F0F0  F2F5F5F6  F5F4F0F0  F2F3F0F2
F2F5F5F4  F3F5F4F0  F2F5F6F2  F2F5F4F7  40404040* F1F5F5F6  F0F0F0F2  F1F1F2F3  F6F5F4F0
F0F5F5F8  F5F4F0F0  F2F6F0F0  40404040  F0F0F0F0  F0F0F0F0  F4F2F0F0  F2F5F2F0  F4F4F7F5
F5F4F7F7  F0F0F0F0  F5F5F4F0  F0F0F0F0  F0F0F0F2  F4F7F0F0  F5F5F2F3  F2F2F0F2  F5F9F9
F7F2F5F0  F2F2F0F2  F2F2F0F2  F0F2F3F5  F4F6F8F7  40404040  F0F2F5    F0F0F0F0  F8F7F4F1
F0F0F0F0  F0F0F0F0  F2F2F0F2  F2F5F2F5  40404040* F0F0F0F0  F4F0F0F0  F2F2F0F2  F0F0F0F0
F3F2F5F0  F3F2F0F2  F3F5F0F0  F0F0F0F0  40404040* F4F0F0F4  F2F2F0F2  F6F5F4F0  F4F4F7F6
F2F2F5F4  F5F6F0F0  F5F4F0F0  F6F4F5F6  F4F0F0F0  F2F5F5F6  F0F0F0F2  F2F2F0F1  F5F9F9
F1F5F2F0  F0F0F0F0  F2F2F0F2  40404040  F2F5F6F0  F5F9F8F0  40404040** F4F4F7F5  F8F7F4F1
F4F4F7F9  F0F0F1F4  F0F2F3F5  F2F5F4F2  F0F2F1F6  40404040  F0F0F0F2  F2F5F6F3  F0F0F0F0
F6F6F0F1  F0F0F0F0  F4F8F0F0  F0F0F0F0  F0F1F7F3  F5F4F0F0  F1F1F2F3  F5F6F1F5  F0F5F4F6
F0F0F1F4  F7F7F7F0  F1F3F5F4  F0F0F0F0  40404040* F2F5F1F0  F2F5F1F0  F5F4F0F0  F1F2F3F0
F2F2F2F2  F0F0F0F0  F5F4F0F0  F6F2F0F3  F8F5F0F2  40404040** F0F0F0F0  F1F1F2F3  F0F0F0F0
F6F6F0F2  F2F2F0F2  F2F5F6F0  40404040  40404040  40404040** F0F0F0F0  F5F4F0F0  F8F7F4F6
F0F0F5F8  F3F0F0F2  F0F0F0F0  F1F1F5F6F0 F0F2F5F8  F0F1F3F5  F0F1F3F5  F1F2F3F0  F0F5F4F6
F0F5F8F7  F7F7F0F2  F5F5F2F0  F6F6F2F0  F2F5F6F0  F8F5F0F1  F8F5F0F1  F2F2F0F2  F8F7F4F1
F0F5F2F5  F9F6F3F2  F2F5F6F8  40404040  40404040  40404040** 40404040** F2F2F0F2  F5F2
```

Figure 3-9 Output from IEBPTPCH when TOTCONV = XE is specified

The JCL

```
//H4UT3$10 JOB  (0642,OSUTXXXXX,BD,201),
//             'DOUG LOWE'
//      EXEC  PGM=IEBPTPCH
//SYSPRINT DD  SYSOUT=A
//SYSUT1   DD  DSN=H4.INVTRAN,
//             DISP=OLD
//SYSUT2   DD  SYSOUT=A
//SYSIN    DD  *
  PRINT MAXFLDS=14
  RECORD FIELD=(5,1,,1),FIELD=(5,6,,8),FIELD=(3,11,,15),          X
         FIELD=(5,14,,20),FIELD=(5,19,,27),FIELD=(4,24,,34),       X
         FIELD=(5,28,,40),FIELD=(5,33,,47),FIELD=(6,36,,54),       X
         FIELD=(6,42,,62),FIELD=(5,48,,70),FIELD=(5,53,,77),       X
         FIELD=(6,58,,84),FIELD=(5,64,,92)
/*
```

Resulting output

```
                                                                        PAGE 0001

01203 10235 000 25640 02645 6015 01564 640000 001654 01520 56105 400016 01540
01687 90089 004 04000 06510 0005 60044 440000 456400 01065 40000 100054 60001
00564 00049 015 60540 03249 8056 98004 048940 089700 09870 06544 560000 54500
05407 89456 000 40000 00013 5468 71510 100000 100000 00000 00000 000000 00000
16874 40026 748 00265 00259 8200 00124 240078 900126 40001 89001 556700 04898
02211 02200 447 00147 00156 0025 50015 154001 230054 60012 30054 800135 40012
08884 00225 111 00258 01470 0396 00256 560025 603655 50025 40058 700568 90025
02541 20254 111 00145 00256 0036 50025 412005 230069 80058 70074 500856 00965
05877 70254 015 20458 05620 3256 40041 025632 025874 10258 96320 258200 00000
05874 41025 025 10000 01254 7896 98501 023658 965230 21452 14587 740002 54125
48795 00000 235 54500 12450 1254 20014 002222 201475 96014 00100 254001 00200
54777 10010 020 05441 00035 6200 10216 200012 202110 00021 00022 000000 00000
10564 00049 015 60540 03249 8056 84001 048940 089700 09870 06544 560000 54500
05874 41025 025 10000 01254 7896 52102 023658 965230 21452 14587 740002 54125
00564 00049 015 60540 03249 8056 98004 048940 089700 09870 56205 560000 54500
02203 20235 000 25640 02645 6025 02564 640000 002654 02520 00000 400026 02540
05407 89456 000 00000 00023 5468 72520 256254 200000 00000 00000 000000 00000
02542 20254 222 00245 00256 0036 50025 422005 230069 80058 70074 500856 00965
54777 20020 020 05441 00035 6200 40042 020012 202110 00022 00022 000000 00000
02203 20235 000 25640 02645 6025 02020 640000 002654 01520 56105 400016 01540
48795 00000 235 54500 22450 2254 59800 002222 201475 96014 00100 254001 00200
02222 02200 447 00256 00256 0025 50015 154001 230054 60012 30054 800135 40012
05877 70254 025 20458 05620 3256 47502 025632 025874 10258 96320 258200 00000
05407 89456 000 00000 00023 5468 72510 156154 100000 00000 00000 000000 00000
02222 02200 447 00247 00156 0025 50015 154001 230054 60012 30054 800135 40012
05877 70254 025 20458 05620 3256 98502 025632 025874 20258 96320 258200 00000
```

Figure 3-10 Printing with formatting using IEBPTPCH

MAXFLDS parameter indicating that 14 FIELD parameters will be
coded. Then, the RECORD statement defines 14 fields in the input
record. None of them require any conversion. The bottom part of the
figure shows the output from this job. As you can see, the listing is
spaced out in a much more readable form than in figures 3-8 and 3-9.

Example 3: Printing two members of a library

Figure 3-11 shows the JCL and control statements required to print
two members of a partitioned data set named H4.COB.COPYLIB. The
PRINT statement says that the input file is partitioned, two MEMBER
statements will be used, and one FIELD statement will be used. Then,
the MEMBER statements identify the members to be printed. Finally,
the RECORD statement indicates that the output data should be
printed as one field of 80 characters. This RECORD statement is
included so the output won't be printed in groups of eight characters.

Example 4: Using the PUNCH statement for a print operation

Figure 3-12 shows an IEBPTPCH job that works in the same way as
the one in figure 3-11. However, instead of a PRINT statement, this
job uses a PUNCH statement. Since the PUNCH statement doesn't
print in groups of eight, no RECORD statement is required for this job.
As a result, many programmers prefer to use the PUNCH statement
when printing 80-byte records. Notice that I directed the output
(SYSUT2) to a printer (SYSOUT = A).

```
//H4UT3$11 JOB   (0642,OSUTXXXXX,BD,201),
//              'DOUG LOWE'
//         EXEC  PGM=IEBPTPCH
//SYSPRINT DD    SYSOUT=A
//SYSUT1   DD    DSN=H4.COB.COPYLIB,
//              DISP=OLD
//SYSUT2   DD    SYSOUT=A
//SYSIN    DD    *
   PRINT   TYPORG=PO,MAXNAME=2,MAXFLDS=1
   MEMBER  NAME=TRREC
   MEMBER  NAME=BFREC
   RECORD  FIELD=(80,1,,1)
/*
```

Figure 3-11   Printing two members using IEBPTPCH

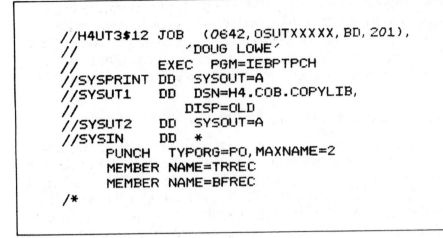

```
//H4UT3$12 JOB   (0642,0SUTXXXXX,BD,201),
//               'DOUG LOWE'
//         EXEC  PGM=IEBPTPCH
//SYSPRINT DD    SYSOUT=A
//SYSUT1   DD    DSN=H4.COB.COPYLIB,
//               DISP=OLD
//SYSUT2   DD    SYSOUT=A
//SYSIN    DD    *
    PUNCH  TYPORG=PO,MAXNAME=2
    MEMBER NAME=TRREC
    MEMBER NAME=BFREC
/*
```

Figure 3-12 Using the PUNCH statement to print two members with IEBPTPCH

DISCUSSION

In addition to the functions presented here, IEBPTPCH provides many more. If you wish to learn about these advanced functions, read the IBM utilities manual. But I don't think there's any reason for you to do that. The material in this chapter should be sufficient for all the IEBPTPCH jobs you'll ever need to run.

As I've already mentioned, many programmers use the IEBGENER utility, described in chapter 2, instead of IEBPTPCH to list the contents of sequential files. Here, I would like to outline the important differences between these two programs:

1. IEBPTPCH always requires control statements. In contrast, IEBGENER can be used without control statements (although the SYSIN DD statement is still required).

2. IEBPTPCH allows you to control the number of lines printed on each page of the output listing. It also lets you print a title at the beginning of the listing and control the output spacing (single, double, or triple spacing). IEBGENER doesn't allow this control.

3. IEBGENER and IEBPTPCH interpret the MEMBER statement differently. For IEBPTPCH, the MEMBER statement refers to a member of the *input* file that is to be printed; for IEBGENER, the MEMBER statement refers to a member of the *output* file that is to be created.

4. IEBPTPCH inserts carriage-control characters in the first byte of each output record; IEBGENER doesn't. However, if the output of IEBGENER is directed to class A output, the operating system will insert a control character in each record automatically.

5. The standard print operation for IEBPTPCH formats the output data into groups of eight characters; the standard operation for IEBGENER does no formatting.

6. If the input record is longer than 132 characters, IEBPTPCH will print it on more than one line. Using IEBGENER, the record will be truncated.

7. IEBGENER allows you to insert a literal value in the output record; IEBPTPCH doesn't.

In general, then, I recommend that you use IEBGENER instead of IEBPTPCH for simple print operations because no control statements are required. Use IEBPTPCH only when necessary (for example, if your input records are over 132 bytes long).

Objective

Given the record layout of a file and a print chart showing the desired output format, create an IEBPTPCH job that will print the file in the desired format.

4

The IEBISAM Utility

The IEBISAM utility program is used to manipulate indexed-sequential (ISAM) files. Specifically, IEBISAM can be used to:

• copy an ISAM file

• unload an ISAM file

• load a previously unloaded ISAM file

• print an ISAM file

The first three functions are commonly used in systems involving ISAM files for two purposes: backup and file reorganization. The last function (printing an ISAM file) is generally used only for testing or debugging purposes.

IEBISAM can be used to back up an ISAM file in one of two ways. First, the ISAM file can be copied, creating another ISAM file. This copy then serves as a backup. The disadvantage of this technique is that since the backup copy is itself an ISAM file, it must be stored on a direct-access volume. So, IEBISAM also provides a method of copying an ISAM file onto a tape. This process is called *unloading*, and the resulting file is called an *unloaded ISAM file*. An unloaded ISAM file is a sequential file that contains the ISAM file's data along with control codes that indicate the index structure of the ISAM file. The unloaded file can then be *loaded* by IEBISAM to recreate the ISAM file. However, you must be aware that an unloaded ISAM file can't be processed like a standard sequential file because of the control codes contained in it. The only thing you can do with an unloaded ISAM file is recreate the original ISAM file using IEBISAM.

IEBISAM is also commonly used to reorganize ISAM files. As an ISAM file is processed, its overflow areas become filled, causing the file to become inefficient to work with. So, when IEBISAM copies or loads an ISAM file, it moves records from the overflow areas into their proper locations in the prime data area.

Keep in mind that IEBISAM can't be used to create an ISAM file from a standard sequential file; the input file must either be an ISAM file or an unloaded version of an ISAM file. To create an ISAM file from a standard sequential file, use the IEBDG utility described in chapter 7.

JCL REQUIREMENTS

Figure 4-1 illustrates the JCL required by the IEBISAM utility. As you can see, the usual DD statements are required: SYSPRINT for the message file, SYSUT1 for the input, and SYSUT2 for the output. However, notice that there is no SYSIN file. Since the operation of IEBISAM is so limited, it is controlled entirely through the PARM operand on the EXEC statement. No control statements are used.

The PARM operand can be coded in one of five ways, as illustrated in figure 4-1. When the first four are used, you don't need to use any quotation marks. Thus,

```
PARM=UNLOAD
```

is an acceptable way to code the PARM operand. However, when the last option is used, you must enclose it in quotes, like this:

```
PARM='PRINTL,N'
```

The quotes are required because of the comma in the PARM field.

When COPY is specified in the PARM operand, IEBISAM simply copies the ISAM file from SYSUT1 to SYSUT2. In this case, both SYSUT1 and SYSUT2 must specify ISAM files (DSORG = IS). The space allocated by the SPACE parameter in the SYSUT2 DD statement must be sufficient to accommodate all of the records in the SYSUT1 file.

UNLOAD means to produce an unloaded version of the ISAM file in a sequential file. Thus, SYSUT1 must specify an ISAM file and SYSUT2 must specify a sequential file. This option is typically used to create a backup copy of an ISAM file on a tape volume.

LOAD means just the opposite of UNLOAD. Instead of reading in an ISAM file and creating an unloaded file, LOAD causes IEBISAM to

```
General format

//stepname EXEC  PGM=IEBISAM,
//               PARM=operation
//SYSPRINT DD   message listing (SYSOUT=A)
//SYSUT1    DD   input file
//SYSUT2    DD   output file

Note: For IEBISAM, there is no SYSIN file.

PARM information on the EXEC statement

COPY          Specifies a copy operation.

UNLOAD        Specifies an unload operation.

LOAD          Specifies a load operation.

PRINTL        Specifies a print operation in hexadecimal format.

'PRINTL,N'    Specifies a print operation in alphanumeric format.
```

Figure 4-1   JCL requirements for the IEBISAM utility

read in a previously unloaded version of an ISAM file and create an
ISAM file from it. In other words, the LOAD option is used to restore
an unloaded ISAM file to its original form.

The PRINTL option causes IEBISAM to print the contents of the
ISAM file specified by SYSUT1 on the device specified by SYSUT2. If
PRINTL is specified, the output is printed in hexadecimal format (two
hexadecimal characters per byte of data). If 'PRINTL,N' is specified,
the output is printed in alphanumeric format—no hexadecimal conversion is done.

IEBISAM EXAMPLES

Now, I'm going to show you several examples of how to use IEBISAM.
Since there are only a few ways to use IEBISAM, these examples
should provide you with a good guide to follow when you create your
own IEBISAM jobs.

Example 1: Copying an ISAM file

Figure 4-2 shows a typical IEBISAM job that makes a backup copy of
an ISAM file. The copy operation is specified by coding COPY in the

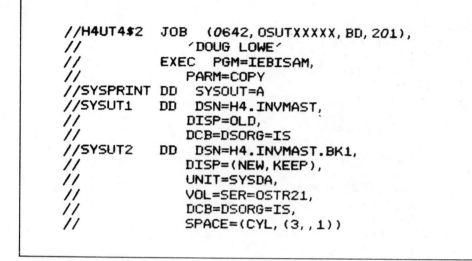

```
//H4UT4$2   JOB   (0642,OSUTXXXXX,BD,201),
//                'DOUG LOWE'
//          EXEC  PGM=IEBISAM,
//                PARM=COPY
//SYSPRINT DD   SYSOUT=A
//SYSUT1   DD   DSN=H4.INVMAST,
//              DISP=OLD,
//              DCB=DSORG=IS
//SYSUT2   DD   DSN=H4.INVMAST.BK1,
//              DISP=(NEW,KEEP),
//              UNIT=SYSDA,
//              VOL=SER=OSTR21,
//              DCB=DSORG=IS,
//              SPACE=(CYL,(3,,1))
```

Figure 4-2   Copying an ISAM file using IEBISAM

PARM field of the EXEC statement. The input file (SYSUT1) is named
H4.INVMAST. The output file (SYSUT2) is named H4.INVMAST.BK1
and will be placed on a volume named OSTR21. The main points to
remember here are that you must specify DSORG = IS on SYSUT1,
and you must specify SPACE, DISP = NEW, and DSORG = IS on
SYSUT2. If you remember these points, a simple copy operation using
IEBISAM should cause you no difficulties.

As IEBISAM copies an ISAM file, it automatically reorganizes it.
In other words, any records stored in overflow areas are moved into
their proper places in the prime data area. Note, however, that it is
the backup copy that is reorganized—not the original file. One way to
reorganize the original ISAM file is to copy it, delete the original
version by specifying DISP = (OLD,DELETE) for SYSUT1, and use the
IEHPROGM utility to assign the original file name to SYSUT2.

Example 2: Unloading and reloading an ISAM file

Although an ISAM file can be reorganized by copying it, as in the last
example, a better way is shown in figure 4-3. Here, the ISAM file is
first unloaded to a tape volume. Since SYSUT1 specifies
DISP = (OLD,DELETE), the ISAM file is deleted after it has been
unloaded. Then, the unloaded version of the file is reloaded, thus
recreating the original ISAM file in a reorganized format. The
unloaded version on the tape volume remains as a backup.

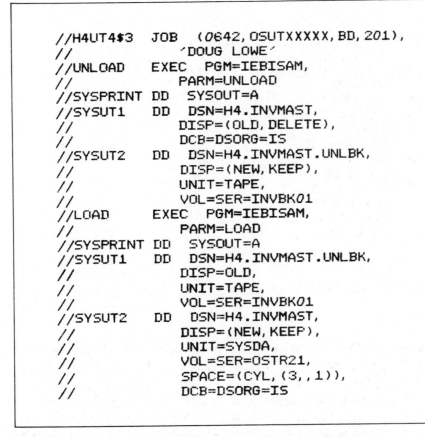

```
//H4UT4$3   JOB   (0642,OSUTXXXXX,BD,201),
//                'DOUG LOWE'
//UNLOAD     EXEC  PGM=IEBISAM,
//                 PARM=UNLOAD
//SYSPRINT DD   SYSOUT=A
//SYSUT1   DD   DSN=H4.INVMAST,
//              DISP=(OLD,DELETE),
//              DCB=DSORG=IS
//SYSUT2   DD   DSN=H4.INVMAST.UNLBK,
//              DISP=(NEW,KEEP),
//              UNIT=TAPE,
//              VOL=SER=INVBK01
//LOAD       EXEC  PGM=IEBISAM,
//                 PARM=LOAD
//SYSPRINT DD   SYSOUT=A
//SYSUT1   DD   DSN=H4.INVMAST.UNLBK,
//              DISP=OLD,
//              UNIT=TAPE,
//              VOL=SER=INVBK01
//SYSUT2   DD   DSN=H4.INVMAST,
//              DISP=(NEW,KEEP),
//              UNIT=SYSDA,
//              VOL=SER=OSTR21,
//              SPACE=(CYL,(3,,1)),
//              DCB=DSORG=IS
```

Figure 4-3 Loading and unloading an ISAM file using IEBISAM

Example 3: Printing an ISAM file

Figure 4-4 shows an IEBISAM job to print the contents of an ISAM file. Because 'PRINTL,N' is specified, the data will be printed in standard alphanumeric format. The output file, SYSUT2, specifies standard printer output (SYSOUT = A). The bottom part of the figure shows how the data appears in the listing. As you can see, the records are automatically identified by the IEBISAM utility. In this case, the records are only 32 bytes long; otherwise, the printed output would extend across the page and continue for as many lines as need-ed for each record.

DISCUSSION

IEBISAM is used primarily for backup and file reorganization pur-poses. Thus, if you are involved in these activities, you need to know

The JCL

```
//H4UT4$4   JOB   (0642,OSUTXXXXX,BD,201),
//               'DOUG LOWE'
//          EXEC  PGM=IEBISAM,
//               PARM='PRINTL,N'
//SYSPRINT  DD    SYSOUT=A
//SYSUT1    DD    DSN=H4.INVMAST,
//               DISP=OLD,
//               DCB=DSORG=IS
//SYSUT2    DD    SYSOUT=A
```

Resulting output

```
    IEBISAM    H4.INVMAST
        RECORD 00001
00509CABLE LOW CAP 1000   000
        RECORD 00002
00510EIA HUB CABLE ASSM   022
        RECORD 00003
005111571 CABLE ASSM      030
        RECORD 00004
03400COUPLER 300 B FULL D002
        RECORD 00005
09010UNIV IO CABLE 8 FT   256
        RECORD 00006
09011UNIV IO CABLE 18 IN 307
             .
             .
             .
        RECORD 00035
094309401 DAA CABLE       027
        RECORD 00036
094319401 3200 CABLE      015
        RECORD 00037
09439RS232 9400 CABLE     023
***END OF OUTPUT
```

Figure 4-4   Printing an ISAM file using IEBISAM

how to use this utility. Another common utility function is creating an ISAM file from a standard sequential file. This is done by using the IEBDG utility, explained in chapter 7.

Terminology

unloading an ISAM file

unloaded ISAM file

loading an ISAM file

Objectives

1. Given a backup or reorganization problem involving ISAM files, create an acceptable IEBISAM job.
2. Given a situation in which you need to print the contents of an ISAM file, write an acceptable IEBISAM job.

(312K)

140K

upervisor

(140K)

5

The IEBCOPY Utility

The IEBCOPY utility is used to make copies of partitioned data sets. Specifically, IEBCOPY can be used to:

• copy a partitioned data set

• compress a partitioned data set

• merge partitioned data sets

In addition, IEBCOPY is capable of selecting or excluding specified members during a copy or merge operation.

Two other utilities are often used to process partitioned data sets. IEBUPDTE is used to make changes in the members of a library or to create or add new members to a library. IEHMOVE can be used to do many of the functions usually done by IEBCOPY; in addition, IEHMOVE can be used to create a backup copy of a partitioned data set on tape in an unloaded format. The IEBUPDTE utility is covered in detail in chapter 6; IEHMOVE is covered in chapter 10.

JCL REQUIREMENTS

Figure 5-1 illustrates the JCL statements required to execute the IEBCOPY utility. As usual, SYSPRINT identifies the message data set and is almost always coded SYSOUT = A. SYSIN contains the control statements and usually indicates instream data (*). Unlike the other utilities, however, IEBCOPY doesn't use SYSUT1 and SYSUT2 to specify

```
//stepname EXEC  PGM=IEBCOPY
//SYSPRINT DD   message file (SYSOUT=A)
//ddname   DD   input file (more than one may be coded)
//ddname   DD   output file
//SYSUT3   DD   work file
//SYSUT4   DD   work file
//SYSIN    DD   control file (usually *)
      control statements
/*
```

Figure 5-1   JCL requirements for the IEBCOPY utility

the input and output files. Instead, you can use any ddnames you want for these files. In the control file, a COPY statement is used to tell the program which files are used for input and which is the output file. You'll see how this works later.

If the input and output files are the same, the library is *compressed*. This means that all of the unused areas in the library are released so they can be used again. It is important to compress libraries frequently because they can run out of space very quickly if you don't.

IEBCOPY requires two work files, so the SYSUT3 and SYSUT4 DD statements must be coded for this utility. These work files don't have to be very big, so in general you only need to assign one track of space to each. I always include a secondary allocation of one track as well, so if the work space exceeds the one track specified in the primary allocation, the program won't have to stop.

CONTROL STATEMENTS

Figure 5-2 shows the control statements IEBCOPY uses. The COPY statement is used to identify the input and output files and is always required. The SELECT and EXCLUDE statements are used if you wish to select or exclude certain members from the copy operation.

To illustrate how the COPY statement is used, consider this example:

```
COPY OUTDD=OUTLIB,INDD=INLIB
```

Here, IEBCOPY will copy the file defined by the DD statement labeled INLIB, creating a file defined by the DD statement labeled OUTLIB. If

---

The COPY statement

```
COPY OUTDD=ddname,INDD=ddname,ddname,...
```

The SELECT statement

```
SELECT MEMBER=membname,membname,...
```

The EXCLUDE statement

```
EXCLUDE MEMBER=membname,membname,...
```

Explanation

OUTDD   Specifies the ddname of the partitioned data set to be created.

INDD   Specifies the ddnames of the input files.

MEMBER   Specifies the names of the members to be selected or excluded.

Figure 5-2   The IEBCOPY control statements

more than one file is identified by the INDD parameter, like this,

```
COPY OUTDD=OUTLIB,INDD=INLIB1,INLIB2
```

the files are copied one after another to create the output file. In other words, the files are merged together. There is no practical limit to the number of input files that may be merged together in an IEBCOPY run.

The SELECT statement is used to select certain members that are to be copied. If a SELECT statement appears in the control file, only the members specified by the SELECT statement are copied to the output file—members that aren't specified are ignored. Notice that the SELECT statement doesn't allow you to specify the name of the library that contains the member. IEBCOPY searches the libraries for the member beginning with the first one you specify in the COPY statement.

The EXCLUDE statement does just the opposite—it causes the specified members to be omitted from the copy operation. If an EXCLUDE statement appears in the control file, all of the members in the input files are copied to the output file except for the ones specified in the EXCLUDE statement. Note that the EXCLUDE and SELECT statements can't be used together. You can use either a SELECT or an EXCLUDE statement—but not both—in the same execution of IEBCOPY.

IEBCOPY EXAMPLES

Now that you have seen the JCL and control statements required for IEBCOPY, I am going to show you some examples of this utility in use.

Example 1: Creating a backup copy of a library

Figure 5-3 shows a basic IEBCOPY setup that creates a backup copy of a partitioned data set. The top part of the figure shows the JCL and control statements. The input file is a cataloged file named H4.COB.COPYLIB. The output file, named H4.COB.COPYLIB.BACKUP, is placed on a backup pack named OSTR21. The COPY statement is used to specify the input and output files. Because this is a simple copy operation, neither the SELECT nor the EXCLUDE statement is used.

The bottom part of figure 5-3 shows the message listing produced by IEBCOPY. This listing contains much useful information. First, it

```
The JCL

//H4UT5$3   JOB   (0642,OSUTXXXXX,BD,201),
//                'DOUG LOWE'
//          EXEC  PGM=IEBCOPY
//SYSPRINT  DD    SYSOUT=A
//COPYLIB   DD    DSN=H4.COB.COPYLIB,
//                DISP=SHR
//BACKLIB   DD    DSN=H4.COB.COPYLIB.BACKUP,
//                DISP=(NEW,CATLG),
//                UNIT=SYSDA,
//                VOL=SER=OSTR21,
//                SPACE=(CYL,(10,1,5)),
//                DCB=(DSORG=PO,RECFM=FB,LRECL=80,BLKSIZE=800)
//SYSUT3    DD    UNIT=SYSDA,
//                SPACE=(TRK,(1,1))
//SYSUT4    DD    UNIT=SYSDA,
//                SPACE=(TRK,(1,1))
//SYSIN     DD    *
     COPY  OUTDD=BACKLIB,INDD=COPYLIB
/*

IEBCOPY message listing

                                   IEBCOPY MESSAGES AND CONTROL STATEMENTS

                    COPY  OUTDD=BACKLIB,INDD=COPYLIB  -
IEB167I  FOLLOWING MEMBER(S) COPIED  FROM INPUT DATA SET REFERENCED BY COPYLIB  -
IEB154I  ARXREC   HAS BEEN SUCCESSFULLY  COPIED
IEB154I  BDREC    HAS BEEN SUCCESSFULLY  COPIED
IEB154I  CRMREC   HAS BEEN SUCCESSFULLY  COPIED
IEB154I  ITRREC   HAS BEEN SUCCESSFULLY  COPIED
IEB154I  OIREC    HAS BEEN SUCCESSFULLY  COPIED
IEB154I  PRODMSTR HAS BEEN SUCCESSFULLY  COPIED
IEB154I  PROMSTR  HAS BEEN SUCCESSFULLY  COPIED
IEB144I  THERE ARE 0000189 UNUSED TRACKS IN OUTPUT DATA SET REFERENCED BY BACKLIB
IEB149I  THERE ARE 0000004  UNUSED DIRECTORY BLOCKS IN OUTPUT DIRECTORY
IEB147I  END OF JOB -00 WAS HIGHEST SEVERITY CODE
```

Figure 5-3   Creating a backup copy of a partitioned data set using IEBCOPY

lists the name of each member that was copied to the output file.
Then, it tells you how much unused space is in the output file. In this
example, there are 189 unused tracks in the data area, and four
unused blocks in the directory. If there is not enough space allocated
for the data area or the directory, these messages will tell you so you
can recode the SPACE parameter in the DD statement and run the job
again.

Example 2: Compressing a partitioned data set

Figure 5-4 shows how IEBCOPY is used to compress a partitioned
data set. Here, the OUTDD and INDD parameters on the COPY
statement specify the same file. After this run, any unused areas in
the library will be released so they can be used again.

The bottom part of this figure shows the outcome of this
compression run. The listing indicates which members were copied to
different locations in the library, and which ones were already
compressed. It also indicates the number of unused tracks and
directory blocks in the library.

```
The JCL

//H4UT5$4   JOB   (0642,OSUTXXXXX,BD,201),
//               'DOUG LOWE'
//               EXEC  PGM=IEBCOPY
//SYSPRINT  DD  SYSOUT=A
//COPYLIB   DD  DSN=H4.COB.COPYLIB,
//               DISP=OLD
//SYSUT3    DD  UNIT=SYSDA,
//               SPACE=(TRK,(1,1))
//SYSUT4    DD  UNIT=SYSDA,
//               SPACE=(TRK,(1,1))
//SYSIN     DD  *
     COPY  OUTDD=COPYLIB,INDD=COPYLIB
/*


IEBCOPY message listing

                              IEBCOPY MESSAGES AND CONTROL STATEMENTS

                     COPY  OUTDD=COPYLIB,INDD=COPYLIB
IEB161I  COMPRESS TO BE DONE USING INDD NAMED COPYLIB
IEB167I  FOLLOWING MEMBER(S) COPIED FROM INPUT DATA SET REFERENCED BY COPYLIB -
IEB154I  ARXREC   HAS BEEN SUCCESSFULLY COPIED
IEB154I  CRMREC   HAS BEEN SUCCESSFULLY COPIED
IEB154I  INVREC   HAS BEEN SUCCESSFULLY COPIED
IEB154I  PRODMSTR HAS BEEN SUCCESSFULLY COPIED
IEB154I  PROMSTR  HAS BEEN SUCCESSFULLY COPIED
IEB144I  THERE ARE 0000189 UNUSED TRACKS IN OUTPUT DATA SET REFERENCED BY COPYLIB
IEB149I  THERE ARE 0000001  UNUSED DIRECTORY BLOCKS IN OUTPUT DIRECTORY
IEB147I  END OF JOB -00 WAS HIGHEST SEVERITY CODE
```

Figure 5-4 A compress-in-place operation using IEBCOPY

Example 3: A selective copy

Figure 5-5 illustrates a selective copy operation. The names of the members in the input file are listed at the top of the figure. Then, the JCL is given. Next, the message listing produced by IEBCOPY is shown. At the bottom of the figure is a listing of the members contained in the new library. In the JCL, the SELECT statement specifies that four members should be copied to the output file. The IEBCOPY message listing indicates that four members of COPYLIB were copied successfully. If you will look at the bottom of the figure, you will see that the members copied to the output file were the ones specified in the SELECT statement.

Example 4: An exclusive copy

Figure 5-6 illustrates an exclusive copy operation. This example uses the same input file as the last example. However, instead of a SELECT statement, an EXCLUDE statement is used to specify that four of the members are not to be copied. If you look at the bottom of the figure, you'll see that all of the members in the input file except those specified in the EXCLUDE statement were copied to the output file.

Example 5: A merge operation

The last example, shown in figure 5-7, is a merge operation. Here, two input libraries (RECLIB and PARLIB) are combined to produce one output library (COPYLIB). The IEBCOPY message listing shows that members were copied from both input libraries. If both libraries contain an identically named member, the member from the last library processed will be included in the new library.

DISCUSSION

IEBCOPY is an important but often neglected utility. The selective/exclusive copy or merge operations are not likely to be required often, but you should use IEBCOPY to reorganize your libraries frequently. Every time you use IEBUPDTE to change the data in a member, the member is copied to a new location in the library. To reclaim the space thus vacated, you must compress the library using IEBCOPY. If you don't, the library will soon run out of space, even though it may contain a great deal of unused space.

Another common use of IEBCOPY is to expand a library. If a library does become filled, new space may be allocated by copying the library. That's when the unused space messages provided by

Members in H4.COB.COPYLIB

```
ARXREC        INVREC
PRODMSTR      BFREC
BDREC         ITRREC
CRMREC        OIREC
PROMSTR       TRREC
```

The JCL

```
//H4UT5$5  JOB  (0642,OSUTXXXXX,BD,201),
//            'DOUG LOWE'
//         EXEC  PGM=IEBCOPY
//SYSPRINT DD  SYSOUT=A
//COPYLIB  DD  DSN=H4.COB.COPYLIB,
//            DISP=OLD
//ARXLIB   DD  DSN=H4.ARXLIB1,
//            DISP=(NEW,CATLG),
//            UNIT=SYSDA,
//            VOL=SER=OSTR21,
//            SPACE=(800,(10,4,4)),
//            DCB=(DSORG=PO,RECFM=FB,LRECL=80,BLKSIZE=800)
//SYSUT3   DD  UNIT=SYSDA,
//            SPACE=(TRK,(1,1))
//SYSUT4   DD  UNIT=SYSDA,
//            SPACE=(TRK,(1,1))
//SYSIN    DD  *
    COPY   OUTDD=ARXLIB,INDD=COPYLIB
    SELECT MEMBER=BDREC,CRMREC,OIREC,ARXREC
/*
```

IEBCOPY message listing

```
                              IEBCOPY MESSAGES AND CONTROL STATEMENTS


                    COPY   OUTDD=ARXLIB,INDD=COPYLIB
                    SELECT MEMBER=BDREC,CRMREC,OIREC,ARXREC
IEB167I  FOLLOWING MEMBER(S)  COPIED  FROM INPUT DATA SET REFERENCED BY COPYLIB  -
IEB154I  ARXREC   HAS BEEN SUCCESSFULLY  COPIED
IEB154I  BDREC    HAS BEEN SUCCESSFULLY  COPIED
IEB154I  CRMREC   HAS BEEN SUCCESSFULLY  COPIED
IEB154I  OIREC    HAS BEEN SUCCESSFULLY  COPIED
IEB144I  THERE ARE 0000000 UNUSED TRACKS IN THE OUTPUT DATA SET REFERENCED BY ARXLIB
IEB149I  THERE ARE 0000003  UNUSED DIRECTORY BLOCKS IN OUTPUT DIRECTORY
IEB147I  END OF JOB -00 WAS HIGHEST SEVERITY CODE
```

Members in H4.ARXLIB1

```
ARXREC        CRMREC
BDREC         OIREC
```

Figure 5-5 A selective copy operation using IEBCOPY

IEBCOPY become important. If you do a compression run on a library and find that there is little or no unused space in the data area or the directory, you should copy the library with IEBCOPY to allocate more space to it.

Members in H4.COB.COPYLIB

```
ARXREC       INVREC
PRODMSTR     BFREC
BDREC        ITRREC
CRMREC       OIREC
PROMSTR      TRREC
```

The JCL

```
//H4UT5$6   JOB   (0642,OSUTXXXXX,BD,201),
//                'DOUG LOWE'
//          EXEC  PGM=IEBCOPY
//SYSPRINT DD   SYSOUT=A
//COPYLIB  DD   DSN=H4.COB.COPYLIB,
//              DISP=OLD
//ARXLIB   DD   DSN=H4.ARXLIB2,
//              DISP=(NEW,CATLG),
//              UNIT=SYSDA,
//              VOL=SER=OSTR21,
//              SPACE=(800,(10,4,4)),
//              DCB=(DSORG=PO,RECFM=FB,LRECL=80,BLKSIZE=800)
//SYSUT3   DD   UNIT=SYSDA,
//              SPACE=(TRK,(1,1))
//SYSUT4   DD   UNIT=SYSDA,
//              SPACE=(TRK,(1,1))
//SYSIN    DD   *
     COPY    OUTDD=ARXLIB,INDD=COPYLIB
     EXCLUDE MEMBER=PRODMSTR,PROMSTR,BFREC,TRREC
/*
```

IEBCOPY message listing

```
                                IEBCOPY MESSAGES AND CONTROL STATEMENTS


                      COPY    OUTDD=ARXLIB,INDD=COPYLIB
                      EXCLUDE MEMBER=PRODMSTR,PROMSTR,BFREC,TRREC
IEB167I  FOLLOWING MEMBER(S) COPIED FROM INPUT DATA SET REFERENCED BY COPYLIB  -
IEB154I  ARXREC    HAS BEEN SUCCESSFULLY  COPIED
IEB154I  BDREC     HAS BEEN SUCCESSFULLY  COPIED
IEB154I  CRMREC    HAS BEEN SUCCESSFULLY  COPIED
IEB154I  INVREC    HAS BEEN SUCCESSFULLY  COPIED
IEB154I  ITRREC    HAS BEEN SUCCESSFULLY  COPIED
IEB154I  OIREC     HAS BEEN SUCCESSFULLY  COPIED
IEB144I  THERE ARE 0000000 UNUSED TRACKS IN THE OUTPUT DATA SET REFERENCED BY ARXLIB
IEB149I  THERE ARE 0000003  UNUSED DIRECTORY BLOCKS IN OUTPUT DIRECTORY
IEB147I  END OF JOB -00 WAS HIGHEST SEVERITY CODE
```

Members in H4.ARXLIB2

```
ARXREC       INVREC
BDREC        ITRREC
CRMREC       OIREC
```

Figure 5-6   An exclusive copy operation using IEBCOPY

Objective

Given a problem that requires copying, compressing, or merging a partitioned data set using IEBCOPY, code the necessary JCL and control statements.

The JCL

```
//H4UT5$7   JOB   (0642,OSUTXXXXX,BD,201),
//              'DOUG LOWE'
//          EXEC  PGM=IEBCOPY
//SYSPRINT  DD    SYSOUT=A
//RECLIB    DD    DSN=H4.COB.RECLIB,
//                DISP=SHR
//PARLIB    DD    DSN=H4.COB.PARLIB,
//                DISP=SHR
//COPYLIB   DD    DSN=H4.COB1.COPYLIB,
//                DISP=(NEW,CATLG),
//                UNIT=SYSDA,
//                VOL=SER=OSTR21,
//                SPACE=(TRK,(10,5,5)),
//                DCB=(DSORG=PO,RECFM=FB,LRECL=80,BLKSIZE=800)
//SYSUT3    DD    UNIT=SYSDA,
//                SPACE=(TRK,(1,1))
//SYSUT4    DD    UNIT=SYSDA,
//                SPACE=(TRK,(1,1))
//SYSIN     DD    *
     COPY   OUTDD=COPYLIB,INDD=RECLIB,PARLIB
/*
```

IEBCOPY message listing

```
                              IEBCOPY  MESSAGES  AND  CONTROL  STATEMENTS


                    COPY     OUTDD=COPYLIB,INDD=RECLIB,PARLIB
IEB167I   FOLLOWING MEMBER(S)  COPIED  FROM INPUT DATA SET REFERENCED BY RECLIB   -
IEB154I   ARREC     HAS BEEN SUCCESSFULLY  COPIED
IEB154I   ARTRANR   HAS BEEN SUCCESSFULLY  COPIED
IEB154I   BDREC     HAS BEEN SUCCESSFULLY  COPIED
IEB154I   BFREC     HAS BEEN SUCCESSFULLY  COPIED
IEB154I   CRMREC    HAS BEEN SUCCESSFULLY  COPIED
IEB154I   INVMSTR   HAS BEEN SUCCESSFULLY  COPIED
IEB154I   OIREC     HAS BEEN SUCCESSFULLY  COPIED
IEB154I   PRODMSTR  HAS BEEN SUCCESSFULLY  COPIED
IEB154I   PROMSTR   HAS BEEN SUCCESSFULLY  COPIED
IEB154I   STATABLE  HAS BEEN SUCCESSFULLY  COPIED
IEB154I   TRREC     HAS BEEN SUCCESSFULLY  COPIED
IEB167I   FOLLOWING MEMBER(S)  COPIED  FROM INPUT DATA SET REFERENCED BY PARLIB   -
IEB154I   ADDWORK   HAS BEEN SUCCESSFULLY  COPIED
IEB154I   AGECALC   HAS BEEN SUCCESSFULLY  COPIED
IEB154I   CHKWRT    HAS BEEN SUCCESSFULLY  COPIED
IEB154I   CONVDATE  HAS BEEN SUCCESSFULLY  COPIED
IEB154I   CONVST    HAS BEEN SUCCESSFULLY  COPIED
IEB154I   DATEDIT   HAS BEEN SUCCESSFULLY  COPIED
IEB154I   MCODER    HAS BEEN SUCCESSFULLY  COPIED
IEB154I   NAMEC     HAS BEEN SUCCESSFULLY  COPIED
IEB154I   STATEDIT  HAS BEEN SUCCESSFULLY  COPIED
IEB144I   THERE ARE 0000009 UNUSED TRACKS IN OUTPUT DATA SET REFERENCED BY COPYLIB
IEB149I   THERE ARE 0000003  UNUSED DIRECTORY BLOCKS IN OUTPUT DIRECTORY
IEB147I   END OF JOB -00 WAS HIGHEST SEVERITY CODE
```

Figure 5-7   A merge operation using IEBCOPY

p

↓ access
device

n

b

j

c

↓ To
direct-
access
device

1
2

→ To

6

The IEBUPDTE Utility

IEBUPDTE is a commonly used utility program that maintains source libraries such as JCL procedure libraries or COBOL COPY libraries. IEBUPDTE can be used to:

• create a new source library

• add a new member to a source library

• catalog a JCL procedure

• change an existing library member

Although IEBUPDTE can perform four other functions, these are the most common.

IEBUPDTE doesn't do all of the library processing functions. For example, it isn't used for making copies of partitioned data sets or for printing the members of a partitioned data set. To copy a library, use the IEBCOPY utility described in chapter 5. To print a member of a library, use the IEBPTPCH utility covered in chapter 3.

JCL REQUIREMENTS

Figure 6-1 illustrates the JCL required to execute IEBUPDTE. As you can see, IEBUPDTE allows you to code the PARM field on the EXEC statement with one of two values: MOD or NEW. If PARM = NEW is specified, IEBUPDTE is used to create a new library. If PARM = MOD is specified

```
//stepname EXEC  PGM=IEBUPDTE [,PARM={MOD }]
                                       {NEW }
//SYSPRINT DD   message listing (SYSOUT=A)
//SYSUT1   DD   existing library
//SYSUT2   DD   new (updated) library
//SYSIN    DD   control file (* or DATA)
      control statements
/*
```

Figure 6-1   JCL requirements for the IEBUPDTE utility

(or if the PARM operand is omitted altogether), IEBUPDTE assumes the library already exists and new members will be added or existing members will be modified.

IEBUPDTE uses the four standard DD statements. SYSPRINT defines the message file and is usually treated as standard printed output (SYSOUT = A). The SYSUT1 and SYSUT2 ddnames describe the source library. Usually, these two DD statements are identical. If a new library is being created (PARM = NEW), no SYSUT1 DD statement is used, and SYSUT2 must specify DISP = NEW. The last DD statement is SYSIN—it defines the control file.

CONTROL STATEMENTS

IEBUPDTE requires two types of control statements: function statements and detail statements. Function statements are used to tell the utility what type of operation is to be performed. Detail statements tell the utility the details of how the individual records are to be manipulated.

For the IEBUPDTE program, all control statements must begin with a period in column 1 and a slash in column 2, like this:

```
./    ADD NAME=TRANREC,LIST=ALL
```

The reason is that the control file may also contain data records (or statements). The period-slash is required to distinguish control statements from data statements.

Function statements

Figure 6-2 gives the formats of the IEBUPDTE function statements. As you can see, there are three different function statements: ADD, CHANGE, and REPLACE. The ADD statement is used to add a new

The ADD statement

```
./ ADD NAME=name,
      LIST=ALL
```

The CHANGE statement

```
./ CHANGE NAME=name,
          LIST=ALL,
          UPDATE=INPLACE
```

The REPLACE statement

```
./ REPL NAME=name,
        LIST=ALL
```

Explanation

NAME	Identifies the name of the member to be processed.
LIST	When LIST = ALL is specified, each updated member is listed along with the control statements. If LIST is omitted, only the control statements and the updated records are listed.
UPDATE	If UPDATE = INPLACE is specified, the library specified by SYSUT2 is updated in its place on the disk—no SYSUT1 DD statement is required. If UPDATE is omitted, SYSUT1 is copied to SYSUT2 as the update is performed.

Figure 6-2   The IEBUPDTE function statements

member to a library (whether the library is being created or already exists); the CHANGE statement is used to change a member by updating its records; and the REPLACE statement is used to change an existing member by completely replacing it with data from the control file.

All three of the function statements require the NAME parameter to specify the name of the member to be processed. In addition, the LIST = ALL parameter may be coded on any of the function statements to indicate that the updated member should be listed on the SYSPRINT file. Since it's a good idea to keep a listing of the latest version of all source members, I always code LIST = ALL on the function statement.

For the CHANGE statement, UPDATE = INPLACE may be coded. When this parameter is used, the library is updated in its place on the disk instead of being copied from SYSUT1 to SYSUT2. Thus, no SYSUT1 DD statement is required. The UPDATE = INPLACE option is useful when the library file is large and requires little maintenance, but it limits the update operations that IEBUPDTE can do. Specifically, IEBUPDTE can only do replace operations that don't change the size of the member if UPDATE = INPLACE is specified—no add, delete, or insert functions can be done.

Detail statements

Figure 6-3 illustrates two of the IEBUPDTE detail statements: NUMBER and DELETE. These statements refer to individual records in the member by specifying *sequence numbers*. These numbers are usually found in columns 73-80 of the source records. Typically, the

---

The NUMBER statement

```
./ NUMBER SEQ1={nnnnnnnn},
              {ALL     }
          SEQ2=nnnnnnnn,
          NEW1=nnnnnnnn,
          INCR=nnnnnnnn,
          INSERT=YES
```

The DELETE statement

```
./ DELETE SEQ1=nnnnnnnn,
          SEQ2=nnnnnnnn
```

Explanation

SEQ1   Specifies the number of the first record to which this detail operation (NUMBER or DELETE) is to apply. If ALL is coded, it specifies that the operation applies to all of the input records. (ALL is only valid on a NUMBER statement.)

SEQ2   Specifies the number of the last record to which this detail operation is to apply. Not valid if SEQ1 = ALL is coded.

NEW1   Specifies the starting number of the updated member. Not used for DELETE.

INCR   Specifies the numbering increment for the updated member. Not used for DELETE.

INSERT   If INSERT = YES is specified, the data records that follow are inserted in the updated library. Not used for DELETE.

Figure 6-3   The IEBUPDTE detail statements

records in a member are numbered beginning with 100 and going up
by tens.

When detail statements are used in conjunction with a CHANGE
statement, IEBUPDTE can do four basic editing functions: (1)
renumber the records in the member, (2) replace records with records
in the control file, (3) insert new records into the member, and (4)
delete records from the member. These functions are illustrated by
figures 6-4 through 6-8.

Renumbering records   Figure 6-4 illustrates how the NUMBER
statement is used to renumber records in a member. As you can see
in the top part of figure 6-4, the original member had records
numbered by tens from 3100 to 3160. The NUMBER statement looks
like this:

```
./    NUMBER    SEQ1=ALL,NEW1=100,INCR=10
```

Because SEQ1 specifies ALL, the renumbering operation will apply to
all of the records in the member. If only certain records were to be

```
TRANREC member before update

    01    TRAN-RECORD.                           00003100
      *                                          00003110
          05    TR-ITEM-NO        PIC  X(5).     00003120
          05    TR-VENDOR-NO      PIC  X(3).     00003130
          05    TR-RECEIPT-DATE   PIC  9(6).     00003140
          05    TR-RECEIPT-QTY    PIC  9(3).     00003150
          05    FILLER            PIC  X(7).     00003160


IEBUPDTE control statements

./   CHANGE    NAME=TRANREC,LIST=ALL
./   NUMBER    SEQ1=ALL,NEW1=100,INCR=10
./   ENDUP


TRANREC member after update

    01    TRAN-RECORD.                           00000100
      *                                          00000110
          05    TR-ITEM-NO        PIC  X(5).     00000120
          05    TR-VENDOR-NO      PIC  X(3).     00000130
          05    TR-RECEIPT-DATE   PIC  9(6).     00000140
          05    TR-RECEIPT-QTY    PIC  9(3).     00000150
          05    FILLER            PIC  X(7).     00000160
```

Figure 6-4   Renumbering a member using IEBUPDTE

renumbered, SEQ1 and SEQ2 would have specified the starting and ending sequence numbers of the records to be renumbered. NEW1 and INCR specify that the new sequence numbers will begin with 100 and count up by tens. A renumbering operation like this is useful when the sequence numbers in a member become unwieldy because complicated changes were made.

Replacing a record   Figure 6-5 shows how a *data statement* is used to replace a record in a member. A data statement is a type of detail statement that contains a sequence number and source data. The source data replaces the data in the record with the same sequence number. As a result of the replacement operation in figure 6-5, the data name TR-ITEM-NO is changed to TR-PART-NO.

Inserting a record   If the sequence number in a data statement doesn't match a record in the member, the source data is inserted in the location indicated by the sequence number, as illustrated in figure 6-6. Since the data statement has a sequence number of 3135, it is inserted between records 3130 and 3140.

```
TRANREC member before update

      01    TRAN-RECORD.                          00003100
      *                                           00003110
            05    TR-ITEM-NO        PIC  X(5).    00003120
            05    TR-VENDOR-NO      PIC  X(3).    00003130
            05    TR-RECEIPT-DATE   PIC  9(6).    00003140
            05    TR-RECEIPT-QTY    PIC  9(3).    00003150
            05    FILLER            PIC  X(7).    00003160

IEBUPDTE control statements

./   CHANGE   NAME=TRANREC,LIST=ALL
            05    TR-PART-NO        PIC  X(5).    00003120
./   ENDUP

TRANREC member after update

      01    TRAN-RECORD.                          00003100
      *                                           00003110
            05    TR-PART-NO        PIC  X(5).    00003120
            05    TR-VENDOR-NO      PIC  X(3).    00003130
            05    TR-RECEIPT-DATE   PIC  9(6).    00003140
            05    TR-RECEIPT-QTY    PIC  9(3).    00003150
            05    FILLER            PIC  X(7).    00003160
```

Figure 6-5   Replacing a record using IEBUPDTE

```
TRANREC member before update

    01   TRAN-RECORD.                             00003100
    *                                             00003110
         05   TR-ITEM-NO          PIC X(5).       00003120
         05   TR-VENDOR-NO        PIC X(3).       00003130
         05   TR-RECEIPT-DATE     PIC 9(6).       00003140
         05   TR-RECEIPT-QTY      PIC 9(3).       00003150
         05   FILLER              PIC X(7).       00003160

IEBUPDTE control statements

./  CHANGE   NAME=TRANREC,LIST=ALL
         05   TR-PURCH-ORD-NO     PIC X(7).       00003135
./  ENDUP

TRANREC member after update

    01   TRAN-RECORD.                             00003100
    *                                             00003110
         05   TR-ITEM-NO          PIC X(5).       00003120
         05   TR-VENDOR-NO        PIC X(3).       00003130
         05   TR-PURCH-ORD-NO     PIC X(7).       00003135
         05   TR-RECEIPT-DATE     PIC 9(6).       00003140
         05   TR-RECEIPT-QTY      PIC 9(3).       00003150
         05   FILLER              PIC X(7).       00003160
```

Figure 6-6 Inserting a record using IEBUPDTE

The NUMBER statement can also be used to insert records into a member, as shown in figure 6-7. Here, the data statements don't have any sequence numbers to indicate where they are to be inserted. Instead, a NUMBER statement is used to specify this information. SEQ1 says to insert the records right after record number 3140. NEW1 and INCR say to number the inserted records beginning with 3150 and going up by tens. INSERT = YES tells the utility that the NUMBER statement is being used for an insertion operation. As you can see in the bottom part of figure 6-7, the records that followed line 3140 in the original member are renumbered following the insertion of the new records. Thus, what used to be record 3150 is now record 3190, and so on.

Deleting records   The DELETE statement is used to delete records from a member, as shown in figure 6-8. In a DELETE statement, SEQ1 and SEQ2 specify a group of records to be deleted. SEQ1 indicates the sequence number of the first record to be deleted, and SEQ2

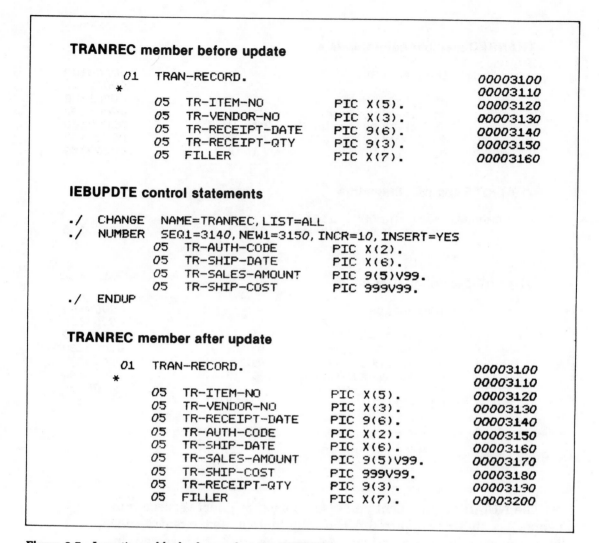

TRANREC member before update

```
01    TRAN-RECORD.                              00003100
 *                                              00003110
      05   TR-ITEM-NO          PIC  X(5).       00003120
      05   TR-VENDOR-NO        PIC  X(3).       00003130
      05   TR-RECEIPT-DATE     PIC  9(6).       00003140
      05   TR-RECEIPT-QTY      PIC  9(3).       00003150
      05   FILLER              PIC  X(7).       00003160
```

IEBUPDTE control statements

```
./   CHANGE    NAME=TRANREC,LIST=ALL
./   NUMBER    SEQ1=3140,NEW1=3150,INCR=10,INSERT=YES
          05   TR-AUTH-CODE        PIC  X(2).
          05   TR-SHIP-DATE        PIC  X(6).
          05   TR-SALES-AMOUNT     PIC  9(5)V99.
          05   TR-SHIP-COST        PIC  999V99.
./   ENDUP
```

TRANREC member after update

```
01    TRAN-RECORD.                              00003100
 *                                              00003110
      05   TR-ITEM-NO          PIC  X(5).       00003120
      05   TR-VENDOR-NO        PIC  X(3).       00003130
      05   TR-RECEIPT-DATE     PIC  9(6).       00003140
      05   TR-AUTH-CODE        PIC  X(2).       00003150
      05   TR-SHIP-DATE        PIC  X(6).       00003160
      05   TR-SALES-AMOUNT     PIC  9(5)V99.    00003170
      05   TR-SHIP-COST        PIC  999V99.     00003180
      05   TR-RECEIPT-QTY      PIC  9(3).       00003190
      05   FILLER              PIC  X(7).       00003200
```

Figure 6-7   Inserting a block of records using IEBUPDTE

indicates the sequence number of the last record to be deleted. Since the DELETE statement in figure 6-8 specifies 3120 for SEQ1 and 3140 for SEQ2, three records will be deleted: 3120, 3130, and 3140.

If you want to delete a single record, simply specify the same number for SEQ1 and SEQ2. For example, consider this DELETE statement:

```
./   DELETE   SEQ1=3110,SEQ2=3110
```

This statement will cause record number 3110 to be deleted. So the DELETE statement can be used to delete a single record as well as a group of records.

```
        TRANREC member before update

            01    TRAN-RECORD.                                      00003100
               *                                                    00003110

                  05    TR-ITEM-NO          PIC  X(5).              00003120
                  05    TR-VENDOR-NO        PIC  X(3).              00003130
                  05    TR-RECEIPT-DATE     PIC  9(6).              00003140
                  05    TR-RECEIPT-QTY      PIC  9(3).              00003150
                  05    FILLER              PIC  X(7).              00003160


        IEBUPDTE control statements

          ./   CHANGE    NAME=TRANREC,LIST=ALL
          ./   DELETE    SEQ1=3120,SEQ2=3140
          ./   ENDUP


        TRANREC member after update

            01    TRAN-RECORD.                                      00003100
               *                                                    00003110

                  05    TR-RECEIPT-QTY      PIC  9(3).              00003150
                  05    FILLER              PIC  X(7).              00003160
```

Figure 6-8   Deleting a block of records using IEBUPDTE

The ENDUP statement

Unlike the other utility programs, IEBUPDTE requires a statement
that indicates the end of the control file: the ENDUP statement. This
must always be the last statement in the control file. It is coded like
this:

```
    ./   ENDUP
```

If the ENDUP statement is omitted, IEBUPDTE will issue an error
message and stop.

IEBUPDTE EXAMPLES

Now that you have seen the utility control statements, I want to show
you some examples of how they are used. So in the pages that follow
are four examples of IEBUPDTE jobs—one for each of the major
IEBUPDTE functions. They are: creating a library, adding a member
to a library, cataloging a procedure, and changing a member.

Example 1: Creating a library

Figure 6-9 shows a typical IEBUPDTE run to create a partitioned data set. Since PARM = NEW is specified on the EXEC statement, no SYSUT1 DD statement is necessary. Instead, SYSUT2 defines the new library, assigning it the name H4.COB.COPYLIB. At the end of the job step, the library will be kept because the DISP operand specifies NEW,KEEP.

In the control file, an ADD statement is used to place one member, named TRANREC, into the library. The NUMBER statement indicates that the member should be numbered by tens beginning with 100. It is followed by data statements containing the actual member. Finally, an ENDUP statement marks the end of the input.

```
The JCL

//H4UT6$9   JOB   (0642,OSUTXXXXX,BD,201),
//                'DOUG LOWE'
//          EXEC  PGM=IEBUPDTE,
//                PARM=NEW
//SYSPRINT DD   SYSOUT=A
//SYSUT2   DD   DSN=H4.COB.COPYLIB,
//                DISP=(NEW,KEEP),
//                UNIT=SYSDA,
//                VOL=SER=OSTR27,
//                SPACE=(TRK,(100,,10),,CONTIG),
//                DCB=(RECFM=F,LRECL=80,BLKSIZE=80)
//SYSIN    DD   *
./         ADD    NAME=TRANREC,LIST=ALL
./         NUMBER NEW1=100,INCR=10
       01  TRAN-RECORD.
      *
           05  TR-ITEM-NO        PIC X(5).
           05  TR-VENDOR-NO      PIC X(3).
           05  TR-RECEIPT-DATE   PIC X(6).
           05  TR-RECEIPT-QTY    PIC 9(3).
           05  FILLER            PIC X(7).
./         ENDUP
/*


The TRANREC member in the source library

       01  TRAN-RECORD.                                00000100
      *                                                00000110
           05  TR-ITEM-NO        PIC X(5).             00000120
           05  TR-VENDOR-NO      PIC X(3).             00000130
           05  TR-RECEIPT-DATE   PIC X(6).             00000140
           05  TR-RECEIPT-QTY    PIC 9(3).             00000150
           05  FILLER            PIC X(7).             00000160
```

Figure 6-9 Creating a source library using IEBUPDTE

Example 2: Adding a member to a source library

Figure 6-10 shows how the IEBUPDTE utility can be used to add a new member to an existing library. As you can see, the SYSUT1 and SYSUT2 DD statements define the same file, so the library will be updated in its original space on the disk. However, bear in mind that the entire library will be processed even if only one member is up-

The JCL

```
//H4UT6$10 JOB    (0642,OSUTXXXXX,BD,201),
//            'DOUG LOWE'
//         EXEC  PGM=IEBUPDTE
//SYSPRINT DD   SYSOUT=A
//SYSUT1   DD   DSN=H4.COB.COPYLIB,
//              DISP=SHR
//SYSUT2   DD   DSN=H4.COB.COPYLIB,
//              DISP=SHR
//SYSIN    DD   *
./    ADD    NAME=BFREC,LIST=ALL
./    NUMBER NEW1=100,INCR=10
          LABEL RECORDS ARE STANDARD
          RECORDING MODE IS F
          RECORD CONTAINS 80 CHARACTERS.

     *
      01   BF-CARD.
     *
          05   BF-ITEM-NO        PIC 9(5).
          05   FILLER            PIC X(20).
          05   BF-UNIT-COST      PIC 999V99.
          05   FILLER            PIC X(10).
          05   BF-ON-HAND        PIC 9(5).
          05   FILLER            PIC X(35).
./    ENDUP
/*
```

The BFREC member in the source library

```
          LABEL RECORDS ARE STANDARD          00000100
          RECORDING MODE IS F                 00000110
          RECORD CONTAINS 80 CHARACTERS.      00000120
     *                                        00000130
      01  BF-CARD.                            00000140
     *                                        00000150
          05   BF-ITEM-NO       PIC 9(5).     00000160
          05   FILLER           PIC X(20).    00000170
          05   BF-UNIT-COST     PIC 999V99.   00000180
          05   FILLER           PIC X(10).    00000190
          05   BF-ON-HAND       PIC 9(5).     00000200
          05   FILLER           PIC X(35).    00000210
```

Figure 6-10   Adding a member to a source library using IEBUPDTE

dated—the other members will simply be copied back into the same disk location. Since DISP = SHR is specified, the library can be accessed by other programs as the new member is being added.

The control statements for this example are identical to those for the last example except that the member name and the source data are different. So the ADD statement is used to add a member to a new library and to an existing library in the same way.

Example 3: Cataloging a JCL procedure

Although cataloging a procedure is really the same as adding a member to a source library, I have provided a separate example because it is such a common function. So in figure 6-11 you can see how it is done. SYSUT1 and SYSUT2 refer to the system procedure

```
The JCL

//H4UT6$11 JOB   (0642,OSUTXXXXX,BD,201),
//              'DOUG LOWE',
//              TYPRUN=HOLD
//          EXEC   PGM=IEBUPDTE
//SYSPRINT DD   SYSOUT=A
//SYSUT1   DD   DSN=H4.PROCLIB,
//              DISP=SHR
//SYSUT2   DD   DSN=H4.PROCLIB,
//              DISP=SHR
//SYSIN    DD   DATA
./     ADD     NAME=E71,LIST=ALL
./     NUMBER NEW1=100,INCR=10
//E71      EXEC   PGM=E71
//STEPLIB  DD   DSN=SYS1.PGMLIB,
//              DISP=SHR
//PARTABLE DD   DSN=E71TOL,
//              UNIT=2400,
//              VOL=SER=E71001,
//              DCB=(RECFM=FB,LRECL=23,BLKSIZE=2300,BUFNO=1),
//              DISP=(OLD,KEEP)
//INVALIST DD   SYSOUT=L,
//              DCB=(RECFM=FBA,LRECL=133,BLKSIZE=2660)
//SYSUDUMP DD   SYSOUT=N
./     ENDUP
/*


The E71 member in the procedure library

//E71      EXEC   PGM=E71                                              00000100
//STEPLIB  DD   DSN=SYS1.PGMLIB,                                       00000110
//              DISP=SHR                                               00000120
//PARTABLE DD   DSN=E71TOL,                                            00000130
//              UNIT=2400,                                             00000140
//              VOL=SER=E71001,                                        00000150
//              DCB=(RECFM=FB,LRECL=23,BLKSIZE=2300,BUFNO=1),          00000160
//              DISP=(OLD,KEEP)                                        00000170
//INVALIST DD   SYSOUT=L,                                             00000180
//              DCB=(RECFM=FBA,LRECL=133,BLKSIZE=2660)                 00000190
//SYSUDUMP DD   SYSOUT=N                                               00000200
```

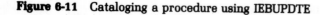

Figure 6-11   Cataloging a procedure using IEBUPDTE

library, H4.PROCLIB, a cataloged file. The DISP is coded SHR so other jobs can use the library while the new procedure is being added. And since the control file contains JCL statements as data, the SYSIN DD statement is coded with the DATA operand.

Example 4: Making changes to an existing member

Figure 6-12 shows an IEBUPDTE run that makes a few simple changes to the procedure added to H4.PROCLIB in the last example. The JCL is similar to that in figure 6-11, except that the DISP field is coded (OLD,KEEP) so the update utility will have exclusive access to the library while it is being modified. Since a data set such as H4.PROCLIB is in constant use during the day in a typical installation, you may have to check your shop standards before you request exclusive access to such a file—there may be a specific time during which such updates are done or you may be required to obtain special clearance before you run the job.

In figure 6-12, three changes are made to the cataloged procedure. First, the STEPLIB DD statement is deleted. Since this DD statement is coded on two JCL cards, the DELETE statement is coded like this:

```
./   DELETE SEQ1=110,SEQ2=120
```

Thus, records 110 and 120 will be deleted. Second, the volume serial number for the PARTABLE file is changed to 240107. This is done by replacing statement 150 with a data statement. Third, a DD statement is inserted to define a file named SYSOUT. This is done by using a data statement to insert the record into the proper location in the member.

DISCUSSION

One thing I want you to be aware of is that IEBUPDTE is not the only—or the best—way to update source library files. Independently developed software packages, such as LIBRARIAN or PANVALET, are used in many shops to maintain source libraries in a more efficient way than IEBUPDTE can. However, these packages are expensive, so not all shops have them. That's why you need to know how to use IEBUPDTE.

Objective

Given a library maintenance job involving the use of IEBUPDTE, code the necessary JCL and control statements.

The JCL

```
//H4UT6$12 JOB  (0642,OSUTXXXXX,BD,201),
//              'DOUG LOWE'
//      EXEC  PGM=IEBUPDTE
//SYSPRINT DD  SYSOUT=A
//SYSUT1   DD  DSN=H4.PROCLIB,
//             DISP=(OLD,KEEP)
//SYSUT2   DD  DSN=H4.PROCLIB,
//             DISP=(OLD,KEEP)
//SYSIN    DD  DATA
./    CHANGE NAME=E71,LIST=ALL
./    DELETE SEQ1=110,SEQ2=120
//             VOL=SER=240107,                    00000150
./    ENDUP                                       00000195
/*
```

IEBUPDTE message listing

```
SYSIN                      NEW MASTER              IEBUPDTE LOG PAGE 0001

./    CHANGE NAME=E71,LIST=ALL
./    DELETE SEQ1=110,SEQ2=120
//E71     EXEC  PGM=E71                            00000100
//STEPLIB DD  DSN=SYS1.PGMLIB,                     00000110  *    DELETED*
//            DISP=SHR                             00000120  *    DELETED*
//PARTABLE DD  DSN=E71TOL,                         00000130
//             UNIT=2400,                          00000140
//             VOL=SER=E71001,                     00000150  *    REPLACED*
//             VOL=SER=240107,                     00000150  *    REPLACEMENT*
//             DCB=(RECFM=FB,LRECL=23,BLKSIZE=2300,BUFNO=1),  00000160
//             DISP=(OLD,KEEP)                     00000170
//INVALIST DD  SYSOUT=L,                           00000180
//             DCB=(RECFM=FBA,LRECL=133,BLKSIZE=2660)  00000190  *    INSERTED*
//SYSOUT  DD  SYSOUT=A                             00000195
./    ENDUP                                        00000200
//SYSUDUMP DD  SYSOUT=N
```

Figure 6-12   Updating a member of a library using IEBUPDTE (part 1 of 2)

Updated member in the procedure library

```
//E71      EXEC  PGM=E71                                       00000100
//PARTABLE DD   DSN=E71TOL.                                    00000130
//              UNIT=2400,                                     00000140
//              VOL=SER=240107,                                00000150
//              DCB=(RECFM=FB,LRECL=23,BLKSIZE=2300,BUFNO=1),  00000160
//              DISP=(OLD,KEEP)                                00000170
//INVALIST DD   SYSOUT=L,                                      00000180
//              DCB=(RECFM=FBA,LRECL=133,BLKSIZE=2660)         00000190
//SYSOUT   DD   SYSOUT=A                                       00000195
//SYSUDUMP DD   SYSOUT=N                                       00000200
```

Figure 6-12 Updating a member of a library using IEBUPDTE (part 2 of 2)

7

The IEBDG Utility

IEBDG, the data generator utility program, can be used to:

• create a sequential or ISAM test file

• load an ISAM file from sequential input

Although the primary purpose of IEBDG is to generate test data, it can also be used to create an ISAM file from a sequential input file—a function IEBISAM can't do.

IEBDG can create an output file in two ways. First, it can create an output file using data from an input file you specify. Or, second, it can generate the data itself based on specifications you provide in control statements. If IEBDG is used to generate test data rather than copy it from an input file, it will vary the data for each output record according to a pattern you specify. For example, you could specify that a three-digit numeric field be given an initial value of zero and be increased by one for each output record. Or, you could define an alphanumeric field with a certain initial value and specify that its value be varied in any of eight different ways.

JCL REQUIREMENTS

Figure 7-1 illustrates the JCL IEBDG requires. As usual, SYSPRINT defines the message listing and SYSIN defines the control file. Instead of SYSUT1 and SYSUT2 for input and output, IEBDG allows you to

```
//stepname EXEC   PGM=IEBDG
//SYSPRINT DD    message listing (SYSOUT=A)
//ddname   DD    input file
//ddname   DD    output file
//SYSIN    DD    control file (*)
      control statements
/*
```

Figure 7-1 JCL requirements for the IEBDG utility

use any names you choose for input and output files. The control statements will tell the utility which files to use. If the output file is ISAM, be sure to specify DCB = DSORG = IS on the DD statement. In addition, the DCB parameter should define the key (RKP and KEYLEN).

CONTROL STATEMENTS

IEBDG uses four control statements. The DSD statement identifies the input and output files. The FD statement defines the contents of each field in the output record. The CREATE statement initiates an IEBDG operation by specifying a number of records to be created and a list of FD fields to include in the records. And the END statement marks the end of the control file. These statements are described in detail in the sections that follow.

The DSD statement

The DSD statement, shown in figure 7-2, must always be the first statement in the control file. It identifies the ddnames of the input and output files. If no input file is used, the INPUT parameter is omitted. Notice that the ddnames must be enclosed in parentheses.

The FD statement

The FD statement, illustrated in figure 7-3, is used to define the contents of the fields in the output records. One FD statement is included for each field to be defined. The first two parameters are always required. NAME supplies the field's name, and LENGTH specifies the field's length. The next two parameters are optional. STARTLOC specifies the field's starting position in the output record; if it is omitted, the field simply starts in the next available position. FILL defines a character to be placed in undefined portions of the field. Usually, FILL isn't used because the entire field will be defined.

The DSD statement

```
DSD  OUTPUT=(ddname)
     INPUT=(ddname)
```

Explanation

OUTPUT   Specifies the ddname of the output file.

INPUT   Specifies the ddname of the input file.

Figure 7-2   The DSD statement

The remaining parameters are used for three functions: (1) to assign an initial value to the field, (2) to specify how IEBDG is to vary the field, and (3) to define the input file that will supply data to the field.

Assigning an initial value to a field   An initial value can be assigned to a field in either of two ways. First, you can use the PICTURE parameter to specify your own value. Second, you can use the FORMAT parameter to specify that an IBM-supplied value be assigned to the field. The PICTURE parameter simply contains a literal value that is placed in the field. PICTURE also specifies the length of that literal. For example,

```
PICTURE=5,'ABCDE'
```

means to put the five characters ABCDE in the field. If you place the letter P before the literal, the value will be converted to packed decimal. To illustrate, this code:

```
FD NAME=PD1,LENGTH=3,PICTURE=5,P'00236'
```

causes the hex characters 00 23 6C to be stored in the field (in a packed decimal field, the last hex digit represents the sign—C or F means positive, D means negative). Notice that the length of the field is three, but the length specified in the PICTURE is 5. To store a negative number, you would include a SIGN parameter, like this:

```
PICTURE=5,P'02433',SIGN=-
```

Here, the hex value of the field will be 02 43 3D.

To use one of the IBM-supplied formats, code the FORMAT parameter. Figure 7-4 shows the values that can be coded for the FORMAT parameter and the data placed in the field for each format. To illustrate, consider this example:

```
FD  NAME=FIELD1,LENGTH=6,FORMAT=AN
```

The FD statement

```
FD NAME=name,
    LENGTH=length,
    STARTLOC=starting-location,
    FILL='fill-character',
    FORMAT=pattern,
    PICTURE=length,[P]'character-string',
    SIGN=sign,
    ACTION=action,
    INDEX=number,
      CYCLE=number,
    INPUT=ddname,
      FROMLOC=number
```

Figure 7-3   The FD statement (part 1 of 2)

This will generate a six-character field containing the characters ABCDEF. The other formats can be used to generate alphabetic, numeric, packed-decimal, and other patterns.

Varying the data in a field   Once you have supplied an initial value to a field, you can vary that value in two ways: by specifying an ACTION parameter or by specifying an INDEX parameter. Although the ACTION parameter can be used to specify one of eight standard actions to be taken on the data in a field, I'm only going to describe two of them here: FX and RP. The others aren't commonly used. FX (fixed) causes the data to remain the same for each record—it is the default if no action is specified. RP (ripple) is used when you want the value of a field to change for each record.

To illustrate the effect of RP, suppose you have a five-byte alphanumeric field. If you supplied the initial value ABCDE through a PICTURE parameter, the ripple would look like this:

```
ABCDE
BCDEA
CDEAB
DEABC
EABCD
ABCDE
```

The cycle then repeats itself for each output record. If the initial

Explanation

NAME	The name of this field (required).
LENGTH	The length of this field (required).
STARTLOC	The starting location. If omitted, next available position is used.
FILL	A character used for each undefined byte. May be a hex constant in the form X'hh' where hh represents two hexadecimal digits, or an alphanumeric character enclosed in quotes.
FORMAT	Specifies an IBM-supplied format. Possible values are listed in figure 7-4.
PICTURE	Specifies a user-supplied picture. Length is the number of characters between the quotes. If P is coded before the literal, the value is packed in the output record.
SIGN	The sign of the field. Code SIGN = − for negative numbers.
ACTION	Specifies what action is to be done to the field for each record. Code ACTION=FX (or simply omit the ACTION parameter) if you want the field to remain fixed throughout the operation. If you want to vary the field for each record, code ACTION=RP.
INDEX	A number to be added to the field for each record.
CYCLE	Used only with INDEX. Specifies how often to add the index value to the field.
INPUT	Specifies an input file that will be used to supply data for this field.
FROMLOC	Used only with INPUT. Specifies the starting position of the data in the input record.

Figure 7-3   The FD statement (part 2 of 2)

value of the field was supplied by an IBM pattern (FORMAT = AN), the ripple would look like this:

```
ABCDE
BCDEF
CDEFG
DEFGH
EFGHI
```

and so on, through all of the characters used by the alphanumeric pattern.

The INDEX parameter is used for numeric fields. It specifies a number that is added to the field for each output record. For example,

```
FD NAME=IND1,LENGTH=4,FORMAT=ZD,INDEX=1
```

FORMAT	Name	Description	Initial value (5-byte field)
AN	Alphanumeric	Letters A-Z, digits 0-9	A B C D E
AL	Alphabetic	Letters A-Z	A B C D E
ZD	Zoned decimal	Digits 0-9	0 0 0 0 1
PD	Packed decimal	Packed number	(Hex) 00 00 00 00 1C
BI	Binary pattern	Binary number	(Hex) 00 00 00 00 01
CO	Collating sequence	Special characters: b.<(+|&!$*);⌐ -/,%_>?:#@'=" letters A-Z, digits 0-9 (where b is one blank)	b.<(+ (where b is one blank)
RA	Random pattern	Random hexadecimal digits	(Hex) 4F 38 2D A5 A0

Figure 7-4   IBM-supplied patterns for IEBDG

causes IEBDG to generate 0001 for the first record, 0002 for the second record, 0003 for the third, and so on.

The CYCLE parameter, used only with the INDEX parameter, controls how often the index value is added to the field. For example, if CYCLE = 3 is coded, the index value is added to the field every third record. CYCLE is useful for generating control breaks in the output data. To illustrate, consider these two FD statements:

```
FD NAME=SLSNO,LENGTH=2,FORMAT=ZD,
     INDEX=1,CYCLE=3
FD NAME=CSTNO,LENGTH=3,FORMAT=ZD,INDEX=1
```

They will generate the following values:

SLSNO	CSTNO
01	001
01	002
01	003
02	004
02	005
02	006
03	007

and so on.

Defining an input file that will supply data for a field   If the data is to come from an input file instead of control statements, an FD statement may be used to move data from one field of the input record to another field in the output record. To do this, you must specify two parameters: INPUT and FROMLOC. INPUT simply identifies the ddname of the input file, and FROMLOC specifies the starting position of the field in the input record.

When an input file is used, you can't vary the contents of the field with an ACTION or INDEX parameter. However, you can mix the fields in the output records by coding some of the fields with data from an input file and other fields with data from PICTURE or FOR-MAT parameters. If the data is simply copied from the input records to the output records, you don't need an FD statement at all—instead, you specify the input file in the CREATE statement.

The CREATE statement

The CREATE statement is used to initiate an IEBDG operation. Its format is shown in figure 7-5. Three parameters are listed: INPUT, NAME, and QUANTITY. INPUT specifies the name of the input file used to create the records. If INPUT is not coded, IEBDG will generate the output data based on the specifications in the other control statements. NAME specifies the names of the fields defined by

---

The CREATE statement

```
CREATE  QUANTITY=number,
        INPUT=ddname,
        NAME=(name,name,...)
```

Explanation

QUANTITY   Specifies how many records to generate.

INPUT   Specifies the name of the file used for input.

NAME   Specifies the names of the fields defined by FD statements to be included in the records.

The END statement

```
END
```

Figure 7-5   The CREATE and END statements

FD statements that are to be included in the output record. If NAME is not coded, the data is copied directly from the input file to the output file. (Note that if an FD statement that included an INPUT parameter is used, an INPUT parameter is also required in the CREATE statement. In other words, the file must be defined in three places: the DSD statement, the FD statement, and the CREATE statement.) The QUANTITY parameter is required only if the input comes solely from the other control statements. It simply specifies the number of output records to be generated by IEBDG.

The END statement

The END statement, shown in figure 7-5, marks the end of a set of control statements. You may then begin another set of control statements, which includes a DSD statement and another set of FD statements. However, in most cases, you will only use one set of control statements, so END will be the last statement in the control file.

IEBDG EXAMPLES

Now that you have seen the individual control statements, I am going to show you two examples of how they work together. Then, you should be able to use IEBDG to generate your own test data.

Example 1: Generating test data for an edit program

Figure 7-6 shows the specifications for a program that edits a file of inventory transactions. Figure 7-7 gives a plan for testing this program. As you can see, the first three test phases are responsible for testing the editing functions of the program. Since these phases require complicated test data, the programmer decided to create the data himself. But the fourth phase in the test plan is to test only the volume conditions—table overflow and page overflow. For this phase, the data generator utility will be used.

Figure 7-8 shows the JCL and control statements necessary to generate the test data for phase 4 of the test plan in figure 7-7. Two output files are produced—H4.TESTPN, which contains the part-number test data, and H4.TESTTRN, which contains the transaction test data. In the control file, two sets of control statements are used.

The first set of control statements in figure 7-8 gives the specifications for generating the part-number table data. The first FD statement defines the part-number field with an initial value of 00001 and indexes it by one for each record. The second FD statement defines the rest of the record, which isn't used by the program, with an alphanumeric pattern.

System flowchart

Record layouts

Valid part number records

Field Name	Part Number	Date of Last Price Change	Unit Cost	Unit Price
Characteristics	X(5)	9(6)	9999V99	9999V99
Position	1-5	6-11	12-17	18-23

Sales transactions

Field Name	Update Code	Tran. Type	Customer Order No.	Order Date	Branch Number	Salesman Number	Customer Number	Quantity	Part Number	Unused
Characteristics	X	9	X(10)	9(6)	X(2)	X(3)	X(5)	9(5)	X(5)	X(4)
Position	1	2	3-12	13-18	19-20	21-23	24-28	29-33	34-38	39-42

Return transactions

Field Name	Update Code	Tran. Type	Customer Memo No.	Return Date	Unused	Quantity	Part Number	Return Authorization Code
Characteristics	X	9	X(10)	9(6)	X(5)	9(5)	X(5)	X(4)
Position	1	2	3-12	13-18	19-23	29-33	34-38	39-42

Figure 7-6   Specifications for an edit program (part 1 of 2)

Editing specifications

Return transactions		Sales transactions	
Validity is:		Validity is:	
ITR-UPDATE-CODE	Must be 'C'	ITR-UPDATE-CODE	Must be 'C'
ITR-TRAN-TYPE	Must be 2	ITR-TRAN-TYPE	Must be 1
ITR-CUST-MEMO-NO	Any data	ITR-CUST-ORDER-NO	Any data
ITR-RETURN-DATE	Numeric with	ITR-ORDER-DATE	Numeric with
ITR-RETURN-DAY	day less than 32	ITR-ORDER-DAY	day less than 32
ITR-RETURN-MONTH	month less than 13	ITR-ORDER-MONTH	month less than 13
ITR-RETURN-YEAR	year = current year or current year − 1	ITR-ORDER-YEAR	year = current year or current year − 1
ITR-CUST-NO	Numeric	ITR-BRANCH-NO	Numeric and less than 25
ITR-QUANTITY	Numeric	ITR-SALESMAN-NO	Numeric
ITR-PART-NUMBER	Numeric with match in the valid-part-number file	ITR-CUST-NO	Numeric
ITR-RETURN-AUTH-CODE	Alphabetic	ITR-QUANTITY	Numeric
		ITR-PART-NUMBER	Numeric with match in the valid-part-number file

Figure 7-6 Specifications for an edit program (part 2 of 2)

Test phase	Data	Data source
1. Valid transactions	Three valid part-number records; two valid transactions, one for each transaction code, and one with the first part number in the table, one with the last part number.	Self
2. Single errors	Invalid transactions that will test all possible causes of invalid fields.	Self
3. Contingencies	Mixed data from test runs 1, 2, and 3; any new records that might cause a contingent error.	Self
4. Page overflow and maximum table size	As many part-number records as the program is supposed to provide for; 150 transactions, with enough invalid transactions to cause page overflow.	Test data generator

Figure 7-7   A test plan for the edit program

The second set of control statements in figure 7-8 generates the data for the inventory transaction file. Two FD statements are used here. The first one defines a fixed value for a valid transaction; the second one defines an invalid transaction (it has an A in the update code byte). Then, two CREATE statements are used. The first one generates 50 records using the FD named GOOD; the second generates 100 records using the FD named BAD. Thus, 50 valid transactions and 100 invalid transactions are generated. Notice how continuation statements are used for the long PICTURE literals.

Example 2: Loading an ISAM file from sequential input

Figure 7-9 shows an IEBDG job that creates an ISAM file from card input. The FD statement specifies that the input is to be copied directly to the output file. Although the IBM manual doesn't specifically say IEBDG can be used to load an ISAM file from sequential input, it works. The only problem with this is that an error message indicating a duplicate key will be generated. You can ignore this message, though, because it is in error. The ISAM file generated will be identical to one generated by a COBOL program.

```
//H4UT7$8  JOB   (0642,OSUTXXXXX,BD,201),
//               'DOUG LOWE'
//        EXEC  PGM=IEBDG
//SYSPRINT DD   SYSOUT=A
//TESTPN   DD   DSN=H4.TESTPN,
//              DISP=(NEW,CATLG),
//              UNIT=SYSDA,
//              VOL=SER=OSTR21,
//              SPACE=(TRK,(1,1)),
//              DCB=(DSORG=PS,RECFM=FB,LRECL=23,BLKSIZE=230)
//TESTTRN  DD   DSN=H4.TESTTRN,
//              DISP=(NEW,CATLG),
//              UNIT=SYSDA,
//              VOL=SER=OSTR21,
//              SPACE=(TRK,(5,5)),
//              DCB=(DSORG=PS,RECFM=FB,LRECL=42,BLKSIZE=420)
//SYSIN    DD   *
  DSD   OUTPUT=(TESTPN)
  FD    NAME=PARTNO,LENGTH=5,FORMAT=ZD,INDEX=1
  FD    NAME=REST,LENGTH=18,FORMAT=AN
  CREATE QUANTITY=100,NAME=(PARTNO,REST)
  END
  DSD   OUTPUT=(TESTTRN)
  FD    NAME=GOOD,LENGTH=42,
        PICTURE=42,'C1XXXXXXXXXXXX01018001010000100012340001'    X
  FD    NAME=BAD,LENGTH=42,
        PICTURE=42,'A1XXXXXXXXXXXX01018001010000100000100001'    X
  CREATE QUANTITY=50,NAME=GOOD
  CREATE QUANTITY=100,NAME=BAD
  END
/*
```

Figure 7-8   Creating the phase-4 test data for the edit program using IEBDG

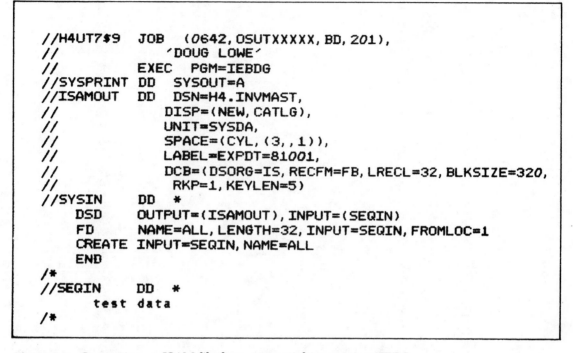

```
//H4UT7$9   JOB   (0642,OSUTXXXXX,BD,201),
//                'DOUG LOWE'
//          EXEC  PGM=IEBDG
//SYSPRINT  DD    SYSOUT=A
//ISAMOUT   DD    DSN=H4.INVMAST,
//                DISP=(NEW,CATLG),
//                UNIT=SYSDA,
//                SPACE=(CYL,(3,,1)),
//                LABEL=EXPDT=81001,
//                DCB=(DSORG=IS,RECFM=FB,LRECL=32,BLKSIZE=320,
//                RKP=1,KEYLEN=5)
//SYSIN     DD  *
    DSD     OUTPUT=(ISAMOUT),INPUT=(SEQIN)
    FD      NAME=ALL,LENGTH=32,INPUT=SEQIN,FROMLOC=1
    CREATE  INPUT=SEQIN,NAME=ALL
    END
/*
//SEQIN     DD  *
     test data
/*
```

Figure 7-9   Generating an ISAM file from sequential input using IEBDG

DISCUSSION

Quite frankly, IEBDG is an awkward way to generate test data. For that reason, I recommend you use it only to generate volume data for testing things like page overflow. For these applications, IEBDG is relatively easy to control. But to generate complex files of test data, it is easier to code the data yourself.

IEBDG is useful for loading ISAM files, though. Usually, to load an ISAM file, you must write a program in COBOL or some other high-level language. Then, you must compile and test that program before you can load the ISAM file. Since IBM has already written that program for you, why not use it? It can save you considerable programming time.

Objective

Given a problem that requires creating a sequential or ISAM file or converting a sequential file to an ISAM file, code an acceptable job using IEBDG.

0 0 0 0 0 0 0 0 0 0 0 0 0 0 0 0 0 0 0 0 0

2 3 4 5 6 7 8 9 10 11 12 13 14 15 16 17 18 19 20 21 22 23 2

1 1 1 1 1 1 1 1 1 1 1 1 1 1 1 1 1 1 1 1 1

2 2 2 2 2 2 2 2 2 2 2 2 2 2 2 2 2 2 2 2 2 2 2 2

3 3 3 3 3 3 3 3 3 3 3 3 3 3 3 3 3 3 3 3 3 3

4 4 4 4 4 4 4 4 4 4 4 4 4 4 4 4 4 4 4 4 4 4 4 4

5 5 5 5 5 5 5 5 5 5 5 5 5 5 5 5 5 5 5 5 5

6 6 6 6 6 6 6 6 6 6 6 6 6 6 6 6 6 6 6 6 6 6 6

7 7 7 7 7 7 7 7 7 7 7 7 7 7 7 7 7 7 7 7 7 7 7 7

8 8 8 8 8 8 8 8 8 8 8 8 8 8 8 8 8 8 8 8 8 8 8 8

8

The IEBCOMPR Utility

IEBCOMPR is a data set utility designed to compare data sets. It can be used to:

- compare sequential data sets
- compare partitioned data sets

Quite simply, IEBCOMPR takes two input files, sequential or partitioned, and compares them. If they are not identical, IEBCOMPR issues a return code of 08 and prints an error message. A return code of zero indicates the files were identical.

This is a simple procedure for standard sequential files. But IEBCOMPR is a little more complicated for partitioned files. In this case, IEBCOMPR only compares members that are common to both libraries. For example, if both libraries contain members named FDREC, GTREC, and DGJREC, then these members will be compared. But a member that appears in only one of the libraries isn't compared. To further complicate matters, IEBCOMPR will signify an unequal comparison if *both* of the libraries contain members that aren't in the other.

In other words, one of the libraries must be a subset of the other for them to be considered equivalent. For example, consider these libraries:

LIB1	LIB2
BFREC	BFREC
BGREC	BGREC
TLREC	TLREC
FJREC	

Here, LIB2 is a subset of LIB1 because all of its members are in LIB1. If the members in LIB2 are identical to the corresponding members in LIB1, IEBCOMPR will indicate an equal comparison (return code = 0). On the other hand, suppose LIB2 contains a member named WSREC. Then, since LIB1 contains a member that isn't in LIB2 (FJREC) and LIB2 contains a member that isn't in LIB1 (WSREC), neither library is a subset of the other so the comparison will be unequal (return code = 08).

JCL REQUIREMENTS

Figure 8-1 illustrates the JCL required by IEBCOMPR. As you can see, SYSPRINT defines the message listing, and SYSUT1 and SYSUT2 define the files that are to be compared. SYSIN is required, but it may be a DUMMY file if the input files are sequential.

CONTROL STATEMENTS

IEBCOMPR uses one control statement, COMPARE. Its format is given in figure 8-2. The only parameter on the COMPARE statement, TYPORG, specifies the organization of the input files. If PO is coded,

```
//stepname EXEC  PGM=IEBCOMPR
//SYSPRINT DD   message listing (SYSOUT=A)
//SYSUT1   DD   input file
//SYSUT2   DD   input file
//SYSIN    DD   control file (* or DUMMY)
      control statements
/*
```

Figure 8-1 JCL requirements for the IEBCOMPR utility

```
The COMPARE statement

COMPARE TYPORG= {PO}
                {PS}
```

Explanation

TYPORG   Specifies the organization of the input file. PO indicates parti-
              tioned organization; PS indicates sequential organization.

Figure 8-2 The COMPARE statement

the files are partitioned. If PS is coded, or if the statement is omitted,
the files are sequential.

IEBCOMPR EXAMPLES

Although IEBCOMPR is not a complicated utility to use, I am going to
present two examples: one compares sequential files, the other compares two libraries.

Example 1: Comparing two sequential files

Figure 8-3 shows an IEBCOMPR job that compares two sequential
files. The JCL here is straightforward. Since the files are sequential,
no control statements are required. So, SYSIN is coded as a DUMMY
file.

The bottom part of figure 8-3 shows the messages printed by
IEBCOMPR as it compares the files. For each unequal comparison,
IEBCOMPR prints this message:

```
IEB221I        RECORDS ARE NOT EQUAL
```

Then it prints the contents of the unequal records in hexadecimal. If
one of the files has more records than the other, IEBCOMPR prints a
message like this:

```
IEB224I        EXTRA RECORD ON SYSUT1
```

followed by a hex listing of the record. (If SYSUT2 contains the extra
record, the message will read EXTRA RECORD ON SYSUT2.)

The last message indicates how many records were compared. If
the files were identical, this would be the only message in the output
listing. Another way to tell if the files were identical is to look at the
completion codes in the JCL listing. A completion code of zero indi-

The JCL

```
//H4UT8$3  JOB  (0642,OSUTXXXXX,BD,201),
//              'DOUG LOWE'
//         EXEC  PGM=IEBCOMPR
//SYSPRINT DD  SYSOUT=A
//SYSUT1   DD  DSN=H4.CPMAST1,
//             DISP=OLD
//SYSUT2   DD  DSN=H4.CPMAST3,
//             DISP=OLD
//SYSIN    DD  DUMMY
```

Resulting output

```
                                       COMPARE UTILITY                                    PAGE  0001

IEB221I    RECORDS ARE NOT EQUAL
    DDNAME = SYSUT1
    PHYSICAL RECORD NUMBER = 00000001  LOGICAL RECORD NUMBER WITHIN PHYSICAL RECORD = 00000001
E2C4C6D3D2D1E2C4C6D3E2D2C4D1C6E2D3C4D2C6D1C1C4D3C6D2E2C4D1C6404040404040404040404040404040404040
404040404040404040404040404040404040
    DDNAME = SYSUT2
    PHYSICAL RECORD NUMBER = 00000001  LOGICAL RECORD NUMBER WITHIN PHYSICAL RECORD = 00000001
C1C4C6D3D2D1D8F4F0C5F9D9C6E2C4D3D1C6D5D8D3E2C5D9E3F0D8F4F8E6F9E4E3D3C5D2D1C6D3D2E2C4D1C6E2D3C4D2C6D1D2404040404040404040404040
4040404040404040404040404040404040404040
IEB221I    RECORDS ARE NOT EQUAL
    DDNAME = SYSUT1
    PHYSICAL RECORD NUMBER = 00000006  LOGICAL RECORD NUMBER WITHIN PHYSICAL RECORD = 00000001
7B5BD99A34D917B5BA3928593933281A28591865D98A65C858691936A29285869187987B5B5C89A399928695A2939286918487864040404040404040404040
404040404040404040404040404040404040
    DDNAME = SYSUT2
    PHYSICAL RECORD NUMBER = 00000006  LOGICAL RECORD NUMBER WITHIN PHYSICAL RECORD = 00000001
C6C1C4E2D3D2C6D1C1E2D3C4D2C6D1E2C4D3C6D2D1E2C4D3C6D2E2D1C4C6D3D2C4D1C6D3E2C4D2C6D1E2C4D3D2C6D1E2C4D3C6404040404040404040404040
4040404040404040404040404040404040404040
IEB224I EXTRA RECORD ON SYSUT1
    DDNAME = SYSUT1
C6C1E2C4F9F8C6E8F4F2D9D1C2E6C5D2D9D1C6C2E2C4D1C8D2C6E5E2C9F7C4F8C6E3E8D8F9C5D9C8D2E6D1C5D9C8E6D2D3D1C5404040404040404040404040
40404040404040404040404040404040404040
    END OF JOB-TOTAL NUMBER OF RECORDS COMPARED = 00000008
```

Figure 8-3 Comparing two sequential files using IEBCOMPR

cates that the files were the same. If the completion code is 08, the files were different.

Example 2: Comparing two partitioned data sets

Figure 8-4 shows a job that compares two partitioned data sets. Since the files are partitioned, a COMPARE statement is included in the control file. The output produced by IEBCOMPR is shown in the bottom part of this figure. In this example, the files were identical. If they were unequal, IEBCOMPR would have printed messages similar to those in figure 8-3.

DISCUSSION

Right now you may be asking this question: Why would anyone want to compare two files? Quite frankly, that's a good question. IEB-COMPR is generally used to verify backup copies created with IEBGENER or IEBCOPY. The chance of either of these programs making an error in copying and not telling you about it is very slight. And, if you assume that IEBGENER or IEBCOPY can make a mistake, how do you know that IEBCOMPR won't make a mistake when it compares the files? In short, most people don't bother to verify backup copies using IEBCOMPR. Sometimes, though, you might need to compare two files that you think might be identical, but you aren't sure. Because these occasions are rare, you probably won't use IEBCOMPR very often.

Objective

Given a problem that requires comparing either sequential data sets or partitioned data sets, code an acceptable job using IEBCOMPR.

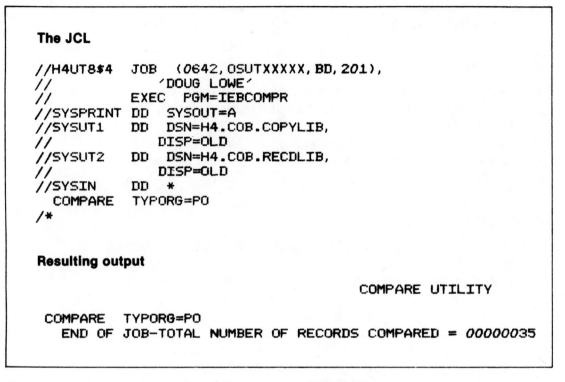

```
The JCL

//H4UT8$4   JOB   (0642,OSUTXXXXX,BD,201),
//               'DOUG LOWE'
//          EXEC  PGM=IEBCOMPR
//SYSPRINT  DD    SYSOUT=A
//SYSUT1    DD    DSN=H4.COB.COPYLIB,
//                DISP=OLD
//SYSUT2    DD    DSN=H4.COB.RECDLIB,
//                DISP=OLD
//SYSIN     DD    *
  COMPARE   TYPORG=PO
/*


Resulting output

                                    COMPARE UTILITY


 COMPARE   TYPORG=PO
    END OF JOB-TOTAL NUMBER OF RECORDS COMPARED = 00000035
```

Figure 8-4   Comparing two partitioned data sets using IEBCOMPR

9

The IEHLIST Utility

IEHLIST is a system utility program that is used to list system data. Specifically, you can use IEHLIST to:

• list the contents of a partitioned data set directory

• list entries in a VTOC

• list entries in a system catalog

Although IEHLIST is classified as a system utility, an applications programmer can frequently use IEHLIST. For example, if you are maintaining a private library containing source programs, you will often want to list the names of the members in the library. Or, if you are using the services of a remote computer installation, you might want a list of all your cataloged files. In short, IEHLIST is a utility you should be familiar with.

JCL REQUIREMENTS

Figure 9-1 illustrates the JCL statements needed to execute the IEHLIST utility. As you can see, the JCL for IEHLIST is a little different than the JCL used by the other utilities. Although SYSPRINT and SYSIN are used for their normal functions (messages and control statements), no SYSUT1 or SYSUT2 DD statements are required. Instead, the DD statements that define the input can have any ddnames you wish. Instead of defining data sets, these DD statements define entire volumes.

```
//stepname EXEC  PGM=IEHLIST
//SYSPRINT DD   message listing (SYSOUT=A)
//ddname   DD   volume containing input file
//SYSIN    DD   control file (*)
      control statements
/*
```

Note: The ddname identifies the volume containing the input file. The DD
statement need only contain UNIT, VOLUME, and DISP parameters.
You may code as many DD statements defining input volumes as
you need.

Figure 9-1   JCL requirements for the IEHLIST utility

The actual data set names of the input files are supplied by utility
control statements. As a result, the input DD statements don't have a
DSN parameter. For example, if you want to list the names of the
members in a library contained on a disk named D00112, you can
code a DD statement like this:

```
//D00112    DD  UNIT=SYSDA,
//              VOL=SER=D00112,
//              DISP=OLD
```

Although the ddname can be any name you choose, I always make it
the same as the volume name so there isn't any confusion.

CONTROL STATEMENTS

IEHLIST has three utility control statements that can be used. They
are illustrated in figure 9-2. The three statements are: LISTPDS, to
list the directory of a partitioned data set; LISTVTOC, to list VTOC
entries; and LISTCTLG, to list entries in a system catalog. As many of
these control statements as you wish may be included in a single
execution of IEHLIST.

The LISTPDS statement

The LISTPDS statement, used to list the directory of a library, has
only two parameters. DSNAME identifies the data set name of the
library, and VOL specifies the volume containing the library. When

The LISTPDS statement

```
LISTPDS  DSNAME=(name,name,...),
         VOL=device=serial
```

The LISTVTOC statement

```
LISTVTOC VOL=device=serial,
         DATE=dddyy,
         DSNAME=(name,name,...),
         FORMAT
```

The LISTCTLG statement

```
LISTCTLG VOL=device=serial,
         NODE=name
```

Explanation

DSNAME   For a LISTPDS statement, DSNAME identifies the data set names of the partitioned data sets whose directories are to be listed. For a LISTVTOC statement, it lists the names of the data sets whose VTOC entries are to be listed. In either case, up to ten names are allowed. The parentheses are required even if only one name is specified.

VOL   Identifies the volume containing the information to be listed. Device corresponds to the UNIT parameter in the DD statement, and serial corresponds to the VOL parameter.

DATE   Specifies a date that is compared with the expiration date for the file. If the file expires before this date, it is flagged with an asterisk in the listing.

NODE   All data sets in the catalog that are qualified by this name are listed. If omitted, all data sets are listed.

FORMAT   Print a formatted listing that includes DSCB and space allocation information. If omitted, an abbreviated listing is produced.

Figure 9-2   The IEHLIST control statements

you code VOL, you include the unit specification as well as the volume name, as in this example:

```
LISTPDS  DSNAME=COPYLIB,VOL=SYSDA=D00112
```

Here, the directory of the library named COPYLIB on disk volume D00112 will be listed. On some systems, a group specification like

SYSDA is not permitted in utility control statements, so you must code
the device type, like this:

```
LISTPDS   DSNAME=COPYLIB,VOL=3330=D00112
```

The volume referenced by the VOL parameter must be described with
a DD statement in the job stream.

The LISTVTOC statement

The LISTVTOC statement is used to list entries in a VTOC. The VOL
parameter is coded just like it is for the LISTPDS statement; it defines
the volume whose VTOC is to be listed. The DATE parameter is used
to cause IEHLIST to check each data set's expiration date (which is
stored in the VTOC) against the date given; if the file has expired, an
asterisk is printed next to it on the listing to indicate that it should be
deleted.

The DSNAME parameter is used to generate a listing of only
selected VTOC entries. For example,

```
LISTVTOC VOL=SYSDA=USER06,
          DSNAME=(WCLIB,WCSPEC)
```

says to list the VTOC entries for the files named WCLIB and WCSPEC
on volume USER06. Notice how the file names are contained in parentheses. The parentheses are required even if only one file name is
listed. You can list up to ten data sets in each LISTVTOC statement;
if you need to list more than that, simply code a second LISTVTOC
statement. If the DSNAME parameter is omitted, all of the entries in
the VTOC are listed.

IEHLIST can print VTOC entries in one of two formats. The first
format lists in detail the information contained in the Data Set
Control Blocks (DSCBs) for the files specified. This includes the data
set name, DCB information like DSORG, RECFM, and BLKSIZE, and
space allocation information. To obtain this output, you must code the
FORMAT parameter on the LISTVTOC statement, like this:

```
LISTVTOC VOL=3330=333005,FORMAT
```

If the FORMAT parameter is omitted, an abbreviated version of the
VTOC entry is printed. The abbreviated version lists only the data set
name, creation and expiration dates, file type, the number of extents,
and a few other items you probably won't need. Since the abbreviated
listing is much easier to work with, I recommend you code the
FORMAT option only if you really need the DCB or allocation
information.

The LISTCTLG statement

To list the system data set catalog, you use the LISTCTLG statement. Like the other utility control statements, LISTCTLG uses the VOL parameter to specify the volume containing the catalog. If you wish to limit your listing to selected files, use the NODE parameter. For example, suppose you only want to list cataloged files that are qualified by the index H4. Then, you would code NODE = H4 on the LISTCTLG statement. If more than one level of qualification is involved, the NODE parameter can be coded like this:

```
NODE=H4.PAY
```

Here, the NODE parameter selects all data sets qualified by PAY within the index H4.

One question you may have is what volume the data set catalog is on. Many installations have several catalog files. If you don't know which volume contains the correct catalog, you can easily find out by looking at the allocation messages from any job that accesses a cataloged file. Somewhere in that listing you will find two messages that look something like this:

```
IEF285I      SYSCTLG.VOCOM25                    KEPT
IEF285I      VOL SER NOS= OCOM25.
```

These messages identify the data set catalog for my system: its name is SYSCTLG.VOCOM25, and it resides on a volume named OCOM25. Although the volume name will probably be different on your system, you should be able to find it in an allocation message like the one listed above.

IEHLIST EXAMPLES

Now that you have seen how the IEHLIST control statements are coded, I want to show you some typical jobs. These examples should provide a clear presentation of how IEHLIST is used.

Example 1: Listing a library directory

The top part of figure 9-3 shows the JCL and control statements required to print the contents of the directory of a partitioned data set named H4.PROCLIB that resides on a volume named OSTR25. You should have no difficulty understanding this job. The DD statement named OSTR25 defines the volume by specifying only the UNIT, VOL, and DISP parameters. Then, the LISTPDS statement is used to specify the volume and the data set name.

```
The JCL

//H4UT9$3  JOB  (0642,0SUTXXXXX,BD,201),
//              'DOUG LOWE'
//         EXEC  PGM=IEHLIST
//SYSPRINT DD  SYSOUT=A
//0STR25   DD  UNIT=SYSDA,
//             VOL=SER=0STR25,
//             DISP=OLD
//SYSIN    DD  *
   LISTPDS DSNAME=(H4.PROCLIB),VOL=3350=0STR25
/*

Resulting output

                          SYSTEMS SUPPORT UTILITIES---IEHLIST

DIRECTORY INFO FOR SPECIFIED PDS ON VOL 0STR25
H4.PROCLIB

      MEMBERS     TTRC              VARIABLE USER DATA ---(USER DATA AND TTRC ARE IN HEX)
      E71         00000700
      PAY04       00000D00
      PAY101      00000A00
      PGC98       00001B00
      PGC97       00001400

OF THE 00005 DIRECTORY BLOCKS ALLOCATED TO THIS PDS, 00004 ARE(IS) COMPLETELY UNUSED
```

Figure 9-3 Listing a PDS directory using IEHLIST

The bottom part of figure 9-3 shows the output from this job. After the heading, the next two lines provide the volume name and the library name. Then, the name of each member and its starting address in hex are provided. The last line of the listing indicates how many directory blocks are unused. (The directory blocks are allocated through the SPACE parameter of the DD statement when the library is created.)

Example 2: Listing the entries of a VTOC

Figure 9-4 shows an example of listing the entries of the VTOC of a disk volume named OSTR27. Here, the entire VTOC is listed in an abbreviated format by using this control statement:

```
LISTVTOC   VOL=SYSDA=OSTR27
```

Again, if your system won't allow you to code a group specification in the utility statement, you will have to code the device type instead.

Figure 9-5 shows the output resulting from this job. In addition to the listing of each file on the volume, IEHLIST tells you how much empty space is on the volume and how many empty entries (blank DSCBs) are available in the VTOC.

Suppose you wanted a detailed VTOC listing of just a few files. Then, you could use the DSNAME parameter of the LISTVTOC statement. To illustrate, consider this statement:

```
LISTVTOC   VOL=3350=OSTR27,
    DSNAME=(H4.INVMAST,H4.ARMAST,
           H4.COB.COPYLIB),
    FORMAT
```

The output generated by this statement is shown in figure 9-6. Using this format IEHLIST can only print three or four data sets on each

```
//H4UT9$4   JOB   (0642,OSUTXXXXX,BD,201),
//                'DOUG LOWE'
//          EXEC  PGM=IEHLIST
//SYSPRINT DD   SYSOUT=A
//OSTR27    DD   UNIT=SYSDA,
//               VOL=SER=OSTR27,
//               DISP=OLD
//SYSIN     DD   *
    LISTVTOC VOL=SYSDA=OSTR27
/*
```

Figure 9-4   Listing the entries of a VTOC using IEHLIST

```
        CONTENTS OF VTOC ON VOL OSTR27                                    PAGE    1
        DATA SET NAME              CREATED  PURGE   FILE TYPE    EXTENTS  FILE SERIAL  VOL. SEQ.  SECURITY
```

SYSTEMS SUPPORT UTILITIES--IEHLIST

DATA SET NAME	CREATED	PURGE	FILE TYPE	EXTENTS	FILE SERIAL	VOL. SEQ.	SECURITY
FN.PROF.LOCK	17278	00000	NOT DEFINED	00000	OSTR27	00001	NONE
BT22.BUDGET	18477	36099	PARTITIONED	00001	&	00001	NONE
SR999.DRSDOC22.DATA	07780	00000	SEQUENTIAL	00001	& ,	00001	NONE
H4.HBFIDK.G0008V00	11680	35099	SEQUENTIAL	00001	&	00001	NONE
SR999.DRSDOC23.DATA	07780	00000	SEQUENTIAL	00001	OSTR27	00001	NONE
FORMAT4.DSCB	17278	00000	NOT DEFINED	00000	& 0	00001	NONE
GH.GHC4.F0000.AA000CYB	24080	36599	SEQUENTIAL	00001	&	00001	NONE
OC43.DATA	19878	35099	SEQUENTIAL	00001	&	00001	NONE
H4.FRFI88.G0994V00	28880	30280	SEQUENTIAL	00001	&	00001	NONE
CP.DAPR201C.G0509V00	29580	35099	SEQUENTIAL	00001	&	00001	NONE
H4.HFFIGS.G0028V00	18480	35099	SEQUENTIAL	00001	&	00001	NONE
BM.CST.I30003B.G0001V00	21180	36099	SEQUENTIAL	00001	& L	00001	NONE
GH.GHCKAAT.PGPROG	14479	36599	SEQUENTIAL	00001	I	00001	NONE
UCW0704.MIF9SOS1.DATA	14480	00000	SEQUENTIAL	00001	&	00001	NONE
H4.TTFI54.G0038V00	24680	36599	SEQUENTIAL	00001	& 6	00001	NONE
H4.WRFIBV.G0877V00	28880	30280	SEQUENTIAL	00001	&	00001	NONE
AC.ACGLDADF.G0007V00	28280	34280	NOT DEFINED	00001	OSTR27	00001	NONE
H4.HR4IGB.G0108V00	24280	36599	SEQUENTIAL	00001	& 2	00001	NONE
H4.HR4IGB.G0113V00	24880	36599	SEQUENTIAL	00001	& 8	00001	NONE
MB.PERM.LOAD.ONLINE	06879	36599	PARTITIONED	00003	b &	00001	NONE
H4.VLTAB2	00979	36099	SEQUENTIAL	00001	I I	00001	NONE
B2OVSO1.WYL.JF.SML.PROCLIB	21179	36099	PARTITIONED	00001	I L	00001	NONE
NG.REL14STD.PHD1D11A.G0076V00	28980	31980	SEQUENTIAL	00001	& A	00001	RACF
GZVSO01.TAPE.JUN80.DATA	19380	36599	SEQUENTIAL	00001	&	00001	NONE
GH.GHMH.F50FJC.SPOOL.G0099V00	29780	36099	SEQUENTIAL	00001	&	00001	NONE
UCW0704.RPM8SSL1.DATA	14880	00000	SEQUENTIAL	00001	& m	00001	NONE
GK.FAMS.MERGED.FILE	31379	36081	SEQUENTIAL	00001	&	00001	NONE
XXX.DSN04	32379	00000	NOT DEFINED	00000	OSTR27	00001	NONE
BA.PRCST001	26879	36599	SEQUENTIAL	00001	I	00001	NONE
H4.FIDN.G0048V00	27780	35099	SEQUENTIAL	00001	&	00001	NONE
UCW0709.EDCP0JL5.DATA	14880	00000	SEQUENTIAL	00001	& m	00001	NONE
TRVS001.PACII.INP.DATA	29580	36599	SEQUENTIAL	00001	& m	00001	NONE
H4.FIGV.G0012V00	13480	35099	SEQUENTIAL	00001	& f	00001	NONE
HKVS001.STAR1.ISI00.DATA	29580	36599	SEQUENTIAL	00007	&	00001	NONE
GH.GHCX.BKUP.F0000.ND300MRF.G0002V00	26880	36599	SEQUENTIAL	00001	&	00001	NONE
BA.PINERDGE.PLOTLIB.M565	11380	36599	PARTITIONED	00001	OSTR27	00001	NONE
H4.HBFIBT.G1706V00	29480	30880	SEQUENTIAL	00001	&	00001	NONE
H4.INVTRN.G0122V00	14880	35099	SEQUENTIAL	00001	& m	00001	NONE
GHCJ001.CMF.DMAP.DATA	07880	36599	SEQUENTIAL	00001	& +	00001	NONE
.							
.							
.							
FN.SMAN.LOCK	20278	20278	NOT DEFINED	00001		00001	NONE
H4.UTFIG8.G0997V00	29180	30580	SEQUENTIAL	00001	&	00001	NONE
H4.UTFIGB.G0156V00	29180	36599	SEQUENTIAL	00001	&	00001	NONE

```
THERE ARE 0035 EMPTY CYLINDERS PLUS 00547 EMPTY TRACKS ON THIS VOLUME
THERE ARE 04199 BLANK DSCBS IN THE VTOC ON THIS VOLUME
```

Figure 9-5 VTOC listing from job shown in figure 9-4

```
                    SYSTEMS SUPPORT UTILITIES---IEHLIST                              PAGE    1

        CONTENTS OF VTOC ON VOL OSTR27

-----DATA SET NAME------------   ID  SER NO  SEQ NO   CREDT   EXPDT   REFDT  NO EXT  DSORG  RECFM  OPTCD  BLKSIZE
H4.INVMAST                        1  OSTR27     1     24280   00181   2428C    3       IS     FB      10     320

   LRECL  KEYLEN  INITIAL ALLOC  2ND ALLOC/LAST BLK PTR(T-R-L)   USED PDS BYTES   FMT 2 OR 3(C-H-R)/DSCB(C-H-R)
     32      5        CYLS                         0                                    0  14  15      0  14  26

   EXTENTS  NO  LOW(C-H)  HIGH(C-H)        NO  LOW(C-H)  HIGH(C-H)
            0   775   0   775  18           1  434   0   435  18    2  776   0   776  18

 2MIND(M-B-C-H)/3MIND(M-B-C-H)/L2MEN(C-H-R)/CYLAD(M-B-C-H)/L3MIN(C-H-R)/ADLIN(M-B-C-H)/ADHIN(M-B-C-H)/NOBYT/ NOTRK
   0  0  0  0   0  0  0  0    0  0  0       0  0  0       0  0  0     3 0 775 18      3 0 775  18   60     0

 LTRAD(C-H-R)/LCYAD(C-H-R)/LMSAD(C-H-R)/LPRAD(M-B-C-H) /NOLEV /CYLOV/ TAGDT/  PRCTR / OVRCT/ RORG1/PTRDS(C-H-R)
   434  0  1   775  18   1   0  0   0  1 0  0  0 1 0 434   43      1       0                37        0    0    0
                            ------UNABLE TO CALCULATE EMPTY SPACE.

-----DATA SET NAME------------   ID  SER NO  SEQ NO   CREDT   EXPDT   REFDT  NO EXT  DSORG  RECFM  OPTCD  BLKSIZE
H4.ARNAST                         1  OSTR27     1     24280   00181   24280    1       PS     FB      00    1000

   LRECL  KEYLEN  INITIAL ALLOC  2ND ALLOC/LAST BLK PTR(T-R-L)   USED PDS BYTES   FMT 2 OR 3(C-H-R)/DSCB(C-H-R)
    100      0        TRKS            10            0 10 2715                           0  13  9       0  13   9

   EXTENTS  NO  LOW(C-H)  HIGH(C-H)
            0   13    0   16   9
                            ------ON THE ABOVE DATA SET, THERE ARE   96 EMPTY TRACK(S).

-----DATA SET NAME------------   ID  SER NO  SEQ NO   CREDT   EXPDT   REFDT  NO EXT  DSORG  RECFM  OPTCD  BLKSIZE
H4.COB.COPYLIB                    1  OSTR27     1     24280   00181   24280    1       PO     FB      00     800

   LRECL  KEYLEN  INITIAL ALLOC  2ND ALLOC/LAST BLK PTR(T-R-L)   USED PDS BYTES   FMT 2 OR 3(C-H-R)/DSCB(C-H-R)
     80      0        TRKS            10            0 15 9945                           0   1  6       0   1   6

   EXTENTS  NO  LOW(C-H)  HIGH(C-H)
            0   12    0   12   9
                            ------ON THE ABOVE DATA SET, THERE ARE    9 EMPTY TRACK(S).
```

Figure 9-6 Formatted VTOC listing produced by IEHLIST

page, so I don't recommend using it unless you select just a few files to be listed.

As you can see, the formatted listing of VTOC entries prints the DSCB and space allocation information stored in the VTOC. Thus, you can determine the file organization, record length, block length, and other information from the listing. For example, the fields highlighted in figure 9-6 show that the file named H4.INVMAST is indexed sequential, has fixed-blocked records, has a block size of 320, and a record size of 32. And, you can see that H4.ARMAST has 96 empty tracks allocated to it.

Although this information is nice to know, I recommend that you don't use IEHLIST just to determine a file's DSCB information. Instead, this information can be determined by looking at the DCB parameter in the job that created the file. So the only time you need to list a VTOC entry with this format is when you need to determine how much empty space is in a file.

Example 3: Listing catalog entries

An example of listing catalog entries is shown in figure 9-7. Here, the catalog resides on a volume named OCOM25. Remember, you can tell what volume the catalog is on by looking for an allocation message for it in the listing from any job that processes a cataloged file. The control statement specifies that only files qualified by the index H4 are to be listed; to list all of the entries in the catalog would only waste paper.

Figure 9-8 shows the output listing from this job. As you can see, IEHLIST lists the following data: file name, the volume containing the file, the file sequence number (which only applies to tape files), and the device type.

```
//H4UTS$7   JOB  (0642,OSUTXXXXX,BD,201),
//               'DOUG LOWE'
//           EXEC  PGM=IEHLIST
//SYSPRINT  DD   SYSOUT=A
//OCOM25    DD   UNIT=SYSDA,
//               VOL=SER=OCOM25,
//               DISP=OLD
//SYSIN     DD   *
    LISTCTLG VOL=SYSDA=OCOM25,NODE=H4
/*
```

Figure 9-7   Listing catalog entries using IEHLIST

```
                        SYSTEMS SUPPORT UTILITIES---IEHLIST


    GENERAL INFORMATION FOR CATALOG ON VOL OCOM25
    DS OR INDEX NAME          ENTRY TYPE          VOL.ID.   SEQ.NO.   DEV.TYPE
      LISTING OF CATALOG BELOW NODE POINT H4
    H4.ARMAST                                     OSTR27    000000    3050200D
    H4.ARXLIB                                     OSTR36    000000    3050200D
    H4.BDG.INVMAST                                OSTR28    000000    3050200D
    H4.BRLIB                                      OSTR36    000000    3050200D
    H4.COB.COPYLIB                                OSTR27    000000    3050200D
    H4.INVMAST                                    OSTR27    000000    3050200D
    H4.INVTRAN                                    OSTR21    000000    3070200D
    H4.PAYFILE                                    OSTR36    000000    3050200D
    H4.PROCLIB                                    OSTR34    000000    3050200D
    H4.PROGLIB                                    OSTR32    000000    3050200D
    H4.LEASFILE.G0001V00                          OSTR28    000000    3050200D
    H4.LEMAST.G0001V00                            OSTR28    000000    3050200D
```

Figure 9-8   Listing of cataloged data sets produced by IEHLIST

DISCUSSION

I want you to be aware that you won't need to use the IEHLIST utility very often. But as I said at the beginning of this chapter, there are times when it is nice to use. You will probably use it most to list PDS directories. Occasionally, you may list a VTOC entry to check its space allocation or DSCB information. And, there are occasions when you might want to check the files cataloged under a particular node qualification. These uses make IEHLIST worth knowing.

Objective

Given a problem that requires listing the contents of a PDS or the contents of either a VTOC or system catalog, code an acceptable job using IEHLIST.

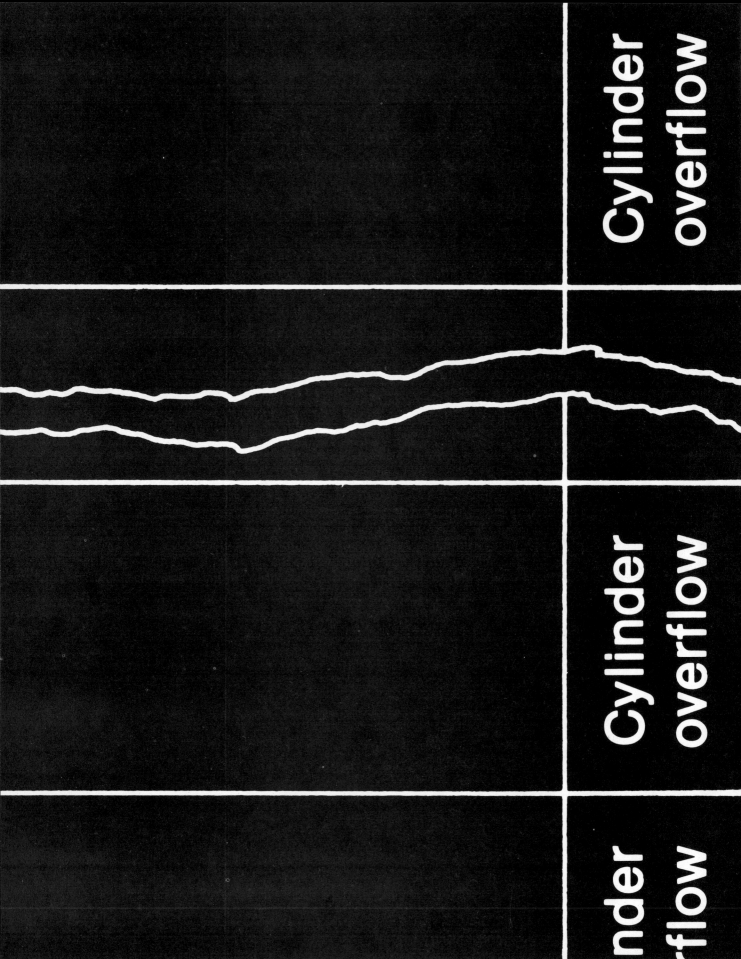

10

The IEHMOVE Utility

IEHMOVE is a utility used to move data sets. You can use it to:

- copy or move a sequential file
- copy or move a partitioned data set
- select, include, or replace members of libraries
- unload partitioned data sets to tape

You may recall that IEBGENER or IEBCOPY can also be used to do some of these functions. The advantage of using IEHMOVE instead is that you don't have to allocate space through the JCL—IEHMOVE automatically allocates space, based on the size of the input file.

Before I show you how to use the IEHMOVE utility, I want to explain the difference between a move and a copy operation. To *copy* a data set means to reproduce it in another location. After a file has been copied, there are two versions of it—the original version and the copy. To *move* a data set, however, means to copy the file and scratch the original, so only one version of the file is left. It's important to remember this distinction when you use IEHMOVE, because you can use the utility to perform either function.

JCL REQUIREMENTS

Figure 10-1 shows the JCL statements needed for IEHMOVE. As usual, SYSPRINT defines the output message file, usually coded SYSOUT = A, and SYSIN defines the control file, usually coded * or DATA. The SYSUT1 DD statement defines a volume on which IEHMOVE can place a temporary work file. Since IEHMOVE will calculate the space required for this file, all you need to code is UNIT, VOLUME, and DISP. For the input and output files, you simply specify the volume—the actual data set name will be supplied by control statements. You can use any ddnames you choose for these DD statements. Since IEHMOVE calculates the space required for the output file, you don't have to specify the SPACE parameter here, either. So, you can code these DD statements the same way you coded the SYSUT1 DD statement—using only UNIT, VOLUME, and DISP.

As you can see in figure 10-1, a DD statement is required to define the system residence volume. Since the volume serial number of the system residence volume varies from one installation to the next, I recommend that you code this DD statement like this:

```
//SYSRES     DD   UNIT=SYSDA,
//                VOL=REF=SYS1.SVCLIB,
//                DISP=OLD
```

Since SYS1.SVCLIB (the supervisor call library) is always cataloged on the system residence volume, this DD statement will work. Although a DD statement to define the system residence volume isn't always required, it's best to include it every time just in case.

```
//stepname EXEC  PGM=IEHMOVE
//SYSPRINT DD    message listing (SYSOUT=A)
//SYSUT1   DD    temporary work file
//ddname   DD    system residence volume
                 (VOL=REF=SYS1.SVCLIB)
//ddname   DD    volume containing input file
//ddname   DD    volume containing output file
//SYSIN    DD    control file (* or DATA)
      control statements
/*
```

Note: The DD statement for the system residence volume may specify
      VOL = REF = SYS1.SVCLIB if you don't know the volume name.

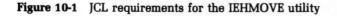

Figure 10-1 JCL requirements for the IEHMOVE utility

CONTROL STATEMENTS

IEHMOVE uses many different control statements. However, in most cases you only need to use a few. In this section, I'm going to cover the COPY, MOVE, SELECT, and EXCLUDE statements as they apply to sequential and partitioned data sets.

The COPY and MOVE statements

The COPY and MOVE statements are used to initiate an IEHMOVE copy or move operation. Although the IBM manual treats the COPY and MOVE statements as separate statements (and it treats them separately for sequential and partitioned files), I am going to treat them together here because they are almost identical. Figure 10-2 shows the combined format of the COPY and MOVE statements. As you might guess, you code a COPY statement to specify a copy operation, and you code a MOVE statement to specify a move operation (in which the original file is scratched). The individual parameters are discussed below.

DSNAME or PDS   These options tell IEHMOVE the name of the file to be copied or moved. If the input file is a sequential or direct data set, code DSNAME. For a partitioned data set, code PDS. If you look in the IBM manual, you will find several other options to code here—DSGROUP, CATALOG, or VOLUME. These options allow you to copy or move a group of data sets, a system catalog, or an entire volume of data sets.

TO   The TO parameter specifies the volume that will receive the new data set. It specifies the device type (such as 3330 or 3350) and the volume serial number.

FROM   The FROM parameter specifies the volume that contains the input file. It is coded like the TO parameter. You don't have to code FROM if the input file is cataloged—IEHMOVE will access the catalog to find the correct volume.

UNCATLG   The UNCATLG option specifies that the catalog entry for the input data set is to be removed from the system catalog. Obviously, this option can be coded only for cataloged data sets. Thus, if you specify the FROM option, the UNCATLG option will be ignored. If the UNCATLG option is omitted, the catalog entry will remain unchanged for copy operations. For a move operation, the catalog entry will be updated so it points to the new volume.

The COPY/MOVE statement

```
(COPY)  (DSNAME=data-set-name)
(MOVE)  (PDS=library-name      ) ,

        TO=device=serial,
        [FROM=device=serial,]
        [UNCATLG,]
        [RENAME=new-name,]
        [EXPAND=number]
```

Explanation

COPY   Specifies a copy operation.

MOVE   Specifies a move operation.

DSNAME   Specifies the input data set (sequential).

PDS   Specifies the input data set (partitioned).

TO   Specifies the output volume.

FROM   Specifies the input volume. Not required if the input file is cataloged.

UNCATLG   Means to uncatalog the input file.

RENAME   Specifies the name of the output file. If omitted, the input file name
           is used.

EXPAND   Specifies a number of 256-byte blocks to be added to the directory
           of a partitioned data set.

Figure 10-2   The COPY/MOVE statement

RENAME   The RENAME parameter is used to change the name of
the data set. If coded, the data set name in the VTOC and in the
system catalog is updated to reflect the name you specify.

EXPAND   The EXPAND parameter, valid only for operations involving partitioned data sets, is used to expand the PDS directory by a
specified number of 256-byte blocks. This option is useful if the directory is full and you need to add additional members to it.

The SELECT and INCLUDE statements

The SELECT and EXCLUDE statements are used to modify a move or
copy operation involving a PDS. They are illustrated in figure 10-3.

The SELECT statement

```
SELECT MEMBER=(name,name,...)
```

The EXCLUDE statement

```
EXCLUDE MEMBER=(name)
```

Explanation

SELECT   Specifies that the listed members are to be included in the output library.

EXCLUDE   Specifies that the listed member is to be excluded from the output library.

MEMBER   The member(s) specified for a select or exclude operation. For a select operation, you must code all of the members to be selected in a single SELECT statement. For an exclude operation, you can code only one member in the EXCLUDE statement, but you may code as many EXCLUDE statements as you need.

Note: You cannot code a SELECT and an EXCLUDE statement together. You can only use one or the other.

Figure 10-3   The SELECT and EXCLUDE statements

The SELECT statement   The SELECT statement is used to limit a move or copy operation involving partitioned data sets to the members specified in the SELECT statement. In other words, if a SELECT statement is coded, only the members specified are moved or copied. Only one SELECT statement may be coded, but you may specify more than one member by separating them with commas and including the list in parentheses, like this:

```
SELECT MEMBER=(ARTREP,TPREP,NOF9)
```

Here, three members are selected for the move or copy operation. You can't use a SELECT statement if you use an EXCLUDE statement.

     The SELECT statement can also assign new names to the members that are selected. To do this, you code the old member name and the new member name together in parentheses, as in this example:

```
SELECT MEMBER=((ARTREP,NEWREP),(TPREP,NPREP))
```

Here, the member named ARTREP is given the new name NEWREP, and TPREP is renamed to NPREP. Notice that if you wish to rename members, you must enclose the list in two sets of parentheses. (Use both sets of parentheses even if only one member is being selected.)

The EXCLUDE statement The EXCLUDE statement is used to exclude certain members from a copy or move operation. The EXCLUDE statement has only one parameter, MEMBER, which specifies the name of the member to be excluded. You may code as many EXCLUDE statements in your control file as you wish. However, you may not use an EXCLUDE statement along with a SELECT statement.

IEHMOVE EXAMPLES

Now that you have seen the format of the IEHMOVE control statements, this section will present several examples so you can see how they work together. For consistency, all of the jobs contain a SYSRES DD statement to define the system residence volume, even though some of the jobs may not require it.

Example 1: Copying a sequential file

Figure 10-4 shows the JCL requirements for making a copy of a sequential file. This job produces the same results as the IEBGENER job in figure 2-4. The input file, H4.INVTRAN, is copied from volume OSTR21 to OSTR36. Since the input file is cataloged, the FROM parameter is omitted from the COPY statement.

```
//H4UT10$4 JOB   (0642,OSUTXXXXX,BD,201),
//              'DOUG LOWE'
//         EXEC  PGM=IEHMOVE
//SYSPRINT DD   SYSOUT=A
//SYSUT1   DD   UNIT=SYSDA,
//              VOL=SER=OSTR31,
//              DISP=OLD
//SYSRES   DD   UNIT=SYSDA,
//              VOL=REF=SYS1.SVCLIB,
//              DISP=OLD
//OSTR21   DD   UNIT=SYSDA,
//              VOL=SER=OSTR21,
//              DISP=OLD
//OSTR36   DD   UNIT=SYSDA,
//              VOL=SER=OSTR36,
//              DISP=OLD
//SYSIN    DD   *
    COPY  DSNAME=H4.INVTRAN,TO=SYSDA=OSTR36
/*
```

Figure 10-4 Copying a sequential file using IEHMOVE

Example 2: Copying a partitioned data set

Figure 10-5 shows an IEHMOVE job that makes a copy of a partitioned data set. This job has the same effect as the IEBCOPY job in figure 5-3. Here, the input library is named H4.COB.COPYLIB, and the output library is renamed to H4.COB.COPYLIB.BACKUP and placed on a disk volume named OSTR21.

Example 3: Backing up a partitioned data set to tape

Figure 10-6 shows an IEHMOVE job that copies a PDS named H4.COB.COPYLIB from a disk volume (OSTR27) to a tape volume (067502). When a library is copied to a tape, it is converted into an *unloaded PDS format.* IEHMOVE can be used to reload the PDS by simply reversing the FROM and TO volumes.

Example 4: Moving a sequential file

Figure 10-7 shows how IEHMOVE can be used to move a sequential file from one volume to another. Here, the file named H4.INVTRAN is moved from volume OSTR27 to volume OSTR21.

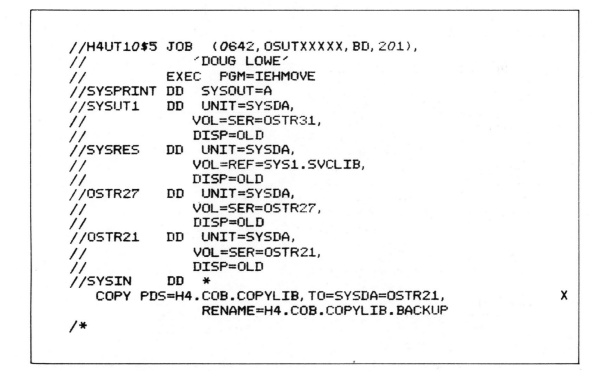

```
//H4UT10$5 JOB  (0642,OSUTXXXXX,BD,201),
//                'DOUG LOWE'
//             EXEC  PGM=IEHMOVE
//SYSPRINT DD   SYSOUT=A
//SYSUT1    DD   UNIT=SYSDA,
//               VOL=SER=OSTR31,
//               DISP=OLD
//SYSRES    DD   UNIT=SYSDA,
//               VOL=REF=SYS1.SVCLIB,
//               DISP=OLD
//OSTR27    DD   UNIT=SYSDA,
//               VOL=SER=OSTR27,
//               DISP=OLD
//OSTR21    DD   UNIT=SYSDA,
//               VOL=SER=OSTR21,
//               DISP=OLD
//SYSIN     DD   *
   COPY PDS=H4.COB.COPYLIB,TO=SYSDA=OSTR21,         X
               RENAME=H4.COB.COPYLIB.BACKUP
/*
```

Figure 10-5   Copying a partitioned data set using IEHMOVE

```
//H4UT10$6 JOB   (0642,OSUTXXXXX,BD,201),
//             'DOUG LOWE'
//             EXEC  PGM=IEHMOVE
//SYSPRINT DD   SYSOUT=A
//SYSUT1    DD   UNIT=SYSDA,
//               VOL=SER=OSTR31,
//               DISP=OLD
//SYSRES    DD   UNIT=SYSDA,
//               VOL=REF=SYS1.SVCLIB,
//               DISP=OLD
//OSTR27    DD   UNIT=SYSDA,
//               VOL=SER=OSTR27,
//               DISP=OLD
//TAPE      DD   DSNAME=H4.COB.COPYLIB,
//               DISP=(NEW,KEEP),
//               UNIT=TAPE,
//               VOL=SER=067502,
//               LABEL=(2,RETPD=030)
//SYSIN     DD   *
  COPY PDS=H4.COB.COPYLIB,TO=TAPE=067502
/*
```

Figure 10-6   Unloading a partitioned data set to a tape volume using IEHMOVE

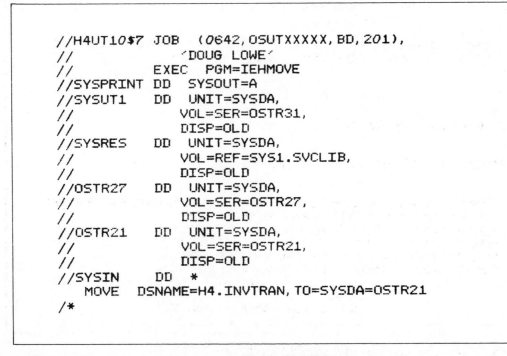

```
//H4UT10$7 JOB   (0642,OSUTXXXXX,BD,201),
//             'DOUG LOWE'
//             EXEC  PGM=IEHMOVE
//SYSPRINT DD   SYSOUT=A
//SYSUT1    DD   UNIT=SYSDA,
//               VOL=SER=OSTR31,
//               DISP=OLD
//SYSRES    DD   UNIT=SYSDA,
//               VOL=REF=SYS1.SVCLIB,
//               DISP=OLD
//OSTR27    DD   UNIT=SYSDA,
//               VOL=SER=OSTR27,
//               DISP=OLD
//OSTR21    DD   UNIT=SYSDA,
//               VOL=SER=OSTR21,
//               DISP=OLD
//SYSIN     DD   *
   MOVE   DSNAME=H4.INVTRAN,TO=SYSDA=OSTR21
/*
```

Figure 10-7   Moving a sequential data set using IEHMOVE

Example 5: A selective copy operation

Figure 10-8 illustrates a selective copy operation. This job works the
same as the IEBCOPY job illustrated in figure 5-5. The SELECT statement specifies that only four of the members in H4.COB.COPYLIB
(BDREC, CRMREC, OIREC, and ARXREC) should be copied. By studying the output generated by IEHMOVE, you can see that only the
desired members were copied into the output library (H4.ARXLIB1).

```
The JCL


//H4UT10$8 JOB   (0642,OSUTXXXXX,BD,201),
//             'DOUG LOWE'
//             EXEC  PGM=IEHMOVE
//SYSPRINT DD   SYSOUT=A
//SYSUT1   DD   UNIT=SYSDA,
//             VOL=SER=OSTR31,
//             DISP=OLD
//SYSRES   DD   UNIT=SYSDA,
//             VOL=REF=SYS1.SVCLIB,
//             DISP=OLD
//OSTR27   DD   UNIT=SYSDA,
//             VOL=SER=OSTR27,
//             DISP=OLD
//OSTR21   DD   UNIT=SYSDA,
//             VOL=SER=OSTR21,
//             DISP=OLD
//SYSIN    DD   *
    COPY PDS=H4.COB.COPYLIB,TO=SYSDA=OSTR21,RENAME=H4.ARXLIB1
    SELECT MEMBER=(BDREC,CRMREC,OIREC,ARXREC)
/*



IEHMOVE message listing


SYSTEM SUPPORT UTILITIES --- IEHMOVE


    COPY PDS=H4.COB.COPYLIB,TO=SYSDA=OSTR21,RENAME=H4.ARXLIB1
    SELECT MEMBER=(BDREC,CRMREC,OIREC,ARXREC)
    MEMBER NAMED BDREC    HAS BEEN MOVED/COPIED.
    MEMBER NAMED CRMREC   HAS BEEN MOVED/COPIED.
    MEMBER NAMED OIREC    HAS BEEN MOVED/COPIED.
    MEMBER NAMED ARXREC   HAS BEEN MOVED/COPIED.
         DATA SET H4.COB.COPYLIB HAS BEEN COPIED TO VOLUME(S)
                  OSTR21
                  AND IS NOW NAMED H4.ARXLIB1
```

Figure 10-8 A selective copy operation using IEHMOVE

Example 6: An exclusive copy operation

Figure 10-9 shows an exclusive copy operation. The EXCLUDE statements specify that four of the members in H4.COB.COPYLIB are to be omitted from the copy operation. Again, by studying the IEHMOVE output you can see that the four members specified were not copied. (This job performs the same type of processing as the IEBCOPY job in figure 5-6.)

DISCUSSION

There are two main advantages to using IEHMOVE instead of IEBGENER or IEBCOPY. First, you only have to code a volume reference in the JCL. If the file you are trying to copy or move doesn't exist, the error will be detected by IEHMOVE instead of by the operating system. Thus, any subsequent job steps will still be executed. If you don't want the rest of the job to execute if the file doesn't exist, you can test the return code generated by IEHMOVE (0 for a successful operation; 12 for an unsuccessful one).

Another advantage of using IEHMOVE is that you don't have to allocate space for the new file in the JCL. Since IEHMOVE allocates space automatically, you don't have to know the size of the files you are copying or moving. Because of this, many programmers prefer to use IEHMOVE instead of IEBGENER or IEBCOPY to copy sequential or partitioned data sets.

Terminology

copy operation

move operation

unloaded PDS format

Objective

Given a problem involving copying or moving a sequential or partitioned data set, code its solution using IEHMOVE.

The JCL

```
//H4UT10$9 JOB  (0642,OSUTXXXXX,BD,201),
//             'DOUG LOWE'
//         EXEC  PGM=IEHMOVE
//SYSPRINT DD  SYSOUT=A
//SYSUT1   DD  UNIT=SYSDA,
//             VOL=SER=OSTR31,
//             DISP=OLD
//SYSRES   DD  UNIT=SYSDA,
//             VOL=REF=SYS1.SVCLIB,
//             DISP=OLD
//OSTR27   DD  UNIT=SYSDA,
//             VOL=SER=OSTR27,
//             DISP=OLD
//OSTR21   DD  UNIT=SYSDA,
//             VOL=SER=OSTR21,
//             DISP=OLD
//SYSIN    DD  *
   COPY PDS=H4.COB.COPYLIB,TO=SYSDA=OSTR21,RENAME=H4.ARXLIB2
   EXCLUDE MEMBER=PRODMSTR
   EXCLUDE MEMBER=PROMSTR
   EXCLUDE MEMBER=BFREC
   EXCLUDE MEMBER=TRREC
/*
```

IEHMOVE message listing

```
SYSTEM SUPPORT UTILITIES --- IEHMOVE


   COPY PDS=H4.COB.COPYLIB,TO=SYSDA=OSTR21,RENAME=H4.ARXLIB2
   EXCLUDE MEMBER=PRODMSTR
   EXCLUDE MEMBER=PROMSTR
   EXCLUDE MEMBER=BFREC
   EXCLUDE MEMBER=TRREC
 MEMBER NAMED ARXREC   HAS BEEN MOVED/COPIED.
 MEMBER NAMED BDREC    HAS BEEN MOVED/COPIED.
 MEMBER NAMED CRMREC   HAS BEEN MOVED/COPIED.
 MEMBER NAMED INVREC   HAS BEEN MOVED/COPIED.
 MEMBER NAMED ITRREC   HAS BEEN MOVED/COPIED.
 MEMBER NAMED OIREC    HAS BEEN MOVED/COPIED.
      DATA SET H4.COB.COPYLIB HAS BEEN COPIED TO VOLUME(S)
                OSTR21
                AND IS NOW NAMED H4.ARXLIB2
```

Figure 10-9 An exclusive copy operation using IEHMOVE

```
                              { ,ddname

rectory) { ,stepname

                              ( ,stepname
```

 allocate to the file as a
n the original file define

11

The IEHPROGM Utility

IEHPROGM is used to modify system control data in the volume table of contents, the data-set label, and the system catalog. Specifically, IEHPROGM can be used to:

- scratch a data set or a member of a partitioned data set
- rename a data set or a member of a partitioned data set
- catalog or uncatalog a data set
- build an index for a generation data group

Although IEHPROGM is capable of performing many other functions, these are the ones most commonly needed by the average programmer.

JCL REQUIREMENTS

Figure 11-1 shows the JCL statements required for the IEHPROGM utility. As usual, SYSPRINT defines the message listing and is usually coded SYSOUT = A, and SYSIN defines the control statement file, usually instream data (*). Instead of the standard SYSUT1 and SYSUT2 DD statements to define input and output files, IEHPROGM requires DD statements to define (1) the volume containing the system catalog and (2) the volume containing the file being processed.

```
//stepname EXEC   PGM=IEHPROGM
//SYSPRINT DD   message listing (SYSOUT=A)
//ddname   DD   volume containing system catalog
//ddname   DD   volume containing data set
//SYSIN    DD   control file (* or DATA)
       control statements
/*
```

Figure 11-1   JCL requirements for the IEHPROGM utility

The DD statements define the volumes only, not the files
themselves. For example,

```
//DD1         DD   UNIT=SYSDA,
//                 VOL=SER=SYSTEM,
//                 DISP=OLD
```

might be an acceptable DD statement to define the system residence
volume for your system. If the catalog is not used in an IEHPROGM
run (for example, a scratch of an uncataloged data set), you don't
have to code a DD statement for the system residence volume.
Similarly, if you aren't actually changing a file (perhaps you are
simply cataloging a file or creating a generation index), you don't
have to include a DD statement to define the volume containing the
file.

If you don't know the name of the volume that contains the
system catalog, you can easily find it by looking at the allocation
messages from any job that accesses a cataloged file. Somewhere in
the listing you will find two messages that look something like this:

```
IEF285I    SYSCTLG.VOCOM25                    KEPT
IEF285I    VOL SER NOS= OCOM25
```

These messages identify the data set catalog from my system: its
name is SYSCTLG.VOCOM25, and it resides on a volume named
OCOM25. Although the name will probably be different on your
system, you should be able to find it in an allocation message like the
one listed above.

CONTROL STATEMENTS

The IEHPROGM utility has 15 control statements that you may use,
but only a few of them are needed most of the time. So, in this section, I'm going to present five common IEHPROGM statements: the

SCRATCH statement to scratch a data set or member, the RENAME statement to change the name of a data set or member, the CATLG and UNCATLG statements to catalog or uncatalog a file, and the BLDG statement to build a generation index for generation data groups. These statements are illustrated in figure 11-2. If by some chance you need to use other IEHPROGM statements, an understanding of these five will make it easier for you to learn the others from the IBM utility manual.

The SCRATCH statement

The SCRATCH statement is used to scratch (delete) a data set or a member of a library. SCRATCH has three parameters: DSNAME, VOL, and MEMBER. The DSNAME specifies the name of the data set to be scratched, or the name of the partitioned data set containing the member to be scratched. The VOL parameter specifies the device type and volume serial number of the volume containing the data set. In your JCL, you must include a DD statement to define this volume. Here's an example of the VOL parameter:

```
VOL=3330=LIB111
```

In this case, the device type is 3330 and the volume serial number is LIB111. On some systems, you can also code a group device name like SYSDA or DISK instead of the actual device number. The MEMBER parameter is used only if a partitioned data set member is to be scratched; it specifies the name of the member.

When IEHPROGM scratches a data set, it doesn't remove it from the system catalog. So, if the data set is cataloged, you should always follow a SCRATCH function by a UNCATLG function. If you don't, you will have an entry in the catalog that points to a file that doesn't exist—a situation that can cause problems.

The RENAME statement

The RENAME statement is used to change the name of a data set or a member in a partitioned data set. RENAME uses four parameters: DSNAME specifies the name of the data set (or the name of the partitioned data set if a member name is to be changed); VOL specifies the device type and volume containing the data set; NEWNAME specifies the new name; and MEMBER specifies the old name of the member if a PDS is being processed. For example,

```
RENAME   DSNAME=MM.ARMAS1,VOL=SYSDA=TESTPK,
         NEWNAME=MM.ARMAST1
```

changes the name of a file from MM.ARMAS1 to MM.ARMAST1.

The SCRATCH statement

```
SCRATCH DSNAME=name,
        VOL=device=serial,
        MEMBER=name
```

The RENAME statement

```
RENAME DSNAME=name,
       VOL=device=serial,
       MEMBER=name,
       NEWNAME=name
```

The CATLG statement

```
CATLG DSNAME=name,
      VOL=device=serial
```

The UNCATLG statement

```
UNCATLG DSNAME=name
```

The BLDG statement

```
BLDG INDEX=name,
     ENTRIES=number,
     {EMPTY }
     {DELETE}
```

Explanation

DSNAME	The name of the data set to be processed.
VOL	The volume containing the data set.
MEMBER	The member name if DSNAME specifies a library.
NEWNAME	The new name of the data set or member that is being renamed.
INDEX	The name of a generation data group.
ENTRIES	The number of generations to be saved in a generation data group.
{EMPTY } {DELETE}	The action to be taken when the generation index is filled. EMPTY means to scratch all entries; DELETE means to scratch only the oldest entry. If both are omitted, the oldest entry is uncataloged but not scratched.

Figure 11-2 The IEHPROGM control statements

Similarly,

```
RENAME   DSNAME=SYS1.COPYLIB,VOL=3330=SYSTEM,
         MEMBER=ARMRED,NEWNAME=ARMREC
```

changes the name of a member in the copy library (SYS1.COPYLIB) from ARMRED to ARMREC.

Like a scratch operation, a rename operation doesn't change the catalog. So, if the data set is cataloged, be sure to include an UNCATLG statement to uncatalog the old name, and a CATLG statement to catalog the file under its new name. Otherwise, you'll have problems later on.

The CATLG statement

The CATLG statement is used to catalog data sets. It uses only two parameters: DSNAME to specify the name of the data set to be cataloged, and VOL to identify the volume containing the data set. To catalog a file, you must include a DD statement in your JCL to identify the volume containing the catalog.

If you are cataloging a tape file, you must specify the data set sequence number in the VOL parameter. For example,

```
CATLG   DSNAME=AMO393,VOL=2400=(TG05,3)
```

means that the file to be cataloged, AMO393, is the third file on tape volume TG05.

The UNCATLG statement

The UNCATLG statement does just the opposite of the CATLG statement: it uncatalogs a file. Only one parameter is required for the UNCATLG statement: DSNAME to specify the name of the file to be removed from the catalog. You don't have to include a DD statement for the file in your JCL, but you do need one to define the volume containing the catalog (usually the system residence volume).

The BLDG statement

The BLDG statement is used to build an index structure in the catalog for generation data groups. There are four parameters used with the BLDG statement. INDEX specifies the name of the generation data group you are defining, and ENTRIES specifies the number of generations you want to keep (1-256). The other two, DELETE and EMPTY, specify what to do when the index structure is filled—that is, the maximum number of generations has been reached. DELETE means that the oldest generation is to be removed from the catalog and

scratched; EMPTY means that *all* of the generations are to be
removed from the catalog (but not scratched). If neither DELETE nor
EMPTY is specified, the oldest generation is removed from the catalog
but not scratched.

IEHPROGM EXAMPLES

Now that you've seen the individual IEHPROGM statements, I'm going
to show you some examples of how they can be used. Then, you'll
have a better perspective on how to use the IEHPROGM utility.

Example 1: Cataloging and uncataloging files

Figure 11-3 gives an example of an IEHPROGM job that catalogs an
ISAM file named H4.INVMAST and uncatalogs a sequential file
named H4.TSTRNS. Only one DD statement is required for this job; it
defines the volume containing the system catalog (usually the system
residence volume). Since the files themselves aren't altered, no DD
statements are required for them.

Example 2: Scratching data sets

Figure 11-4 shows an IEHPROGM job that scratches two data sets:
one named H4.TPAL04, the other named H4.AR.MAST04. Since
H4.AR.MAST04 is cataloged, an UNCATLG statement is included to
uncatalog it. Otherwise, an error will occur if the file is accessed
through the catalog because the file no longer exists. There are two

```
//H4UT11$3 JOB   (0642,OSUTXXXXX,BD,201),
//              'DOUG LOWE'
//          EXEC  PGM=IEHPROGM
//SYSPRINT DD   SYSOUT=A
//OCOM25   DD   UNIT=SYSDA,
//              VOL=SER=OCOM25,
//              DISP=OLD
//SYSIN    DD   *
  CATLG     DSNAME=H4.INVMAST,                        X
            VOL=SYSDA=OSTR34
  UNCATLG   DSNAME=H4.TSTRNS
/*
```

Figure 11-3   Cataloging and uncataloging using IEHPROGM

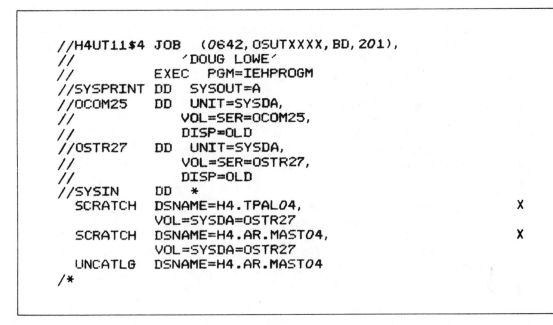

```
//H4UT11$4 JOB  (0642,OSUTXXXX,BD,201),
//              'DOUG LOWE'
//         EXEC  PGM=IEHPROGM
//SYSPRINT DD   SYSOUT=A
//OCOM25   DD   UNIT=SYSDA,
//              VOL=SER=OCOM25,
//              DISP=OLD
//OSTR27   DD   UNIT=SYSDA,
//              VOL=SER=OSTR27,
//              DISP=OLD
//SYSIN    DD   *
   SCRATCH  DSNAME=H4.TPAL04,                    X
            VOL=SYSDA=OSTR27
   SCRATCH  DSNAME=H4.AR.MAST04,                 X
            VOL=SYSDA=OSTR27
   UNCATLG  DSNAME=H4.AR.MAST04
/*
```

Figure 11-4   Scratching data sets using IEHPROGM

DD statements in this example: one defines the system residence volume (OCOM25), the other the volume containing the two files (OSTR27).

Example 3: Renaming a data set

Figure 11-5 shows an example of how to rename a data set. The data set is on a disk volume named OSTR31. Its old name is H4.VLTRANS, and the new name is H4.VALTRAN. Since this operation involves uncataloging the old name and cataloging the file under the new name, both an UNCATLG statement and a CATLG statement are used, and a DD statement is included for the system residence volume (OCOM25).

Example 4: Building a generation index

Figure 11-6 shows an example of creating an index structure for a generation data group. Here, a DD statement for the system residence volume is required (OCOM25). The BLDG statement specifies that the name of the generation data group is H4.ARMAST, that five generations are to be kept, and that the oldest generation is to be scratched when the index is full.

```
//H4UT11$5 JOB   (0642,OSUTXXXXX,BD,201),
//               'DOUG LOWE'
//          EXEC  PGM=IEHPROGM
//SYSPRINT DD   SYSOUT=A
//OCOM25   DD   UNIT=SYSDA,
//              VOL=SER=OCOM25,
//              DISP=OLD
//OSTR31   DD   UNIT=SYSDA,
//              VOL=SER=OSTR31,
//              DISP=OLD
//SYSIN    DD  *
  RENAME    DSNAME=H4.VLTRANS,                               X
            VOL=SYSDA=OSTR31,                                X
            NEWNAME=H4.VALTRAN
  UNCATLG   DSNAME=H4.VLTRANS
  CATLG     DSNAME=H4.VALTRAN,                               X
            VOL=SYSDA=OSTR31
/*
```

Figure 11-5   Renaming a disk file using IEHPROGM

DISCUSSION

As you may have noticed, several of the functions performed by
IEHPROGM are duplicated by other utilities. For example, you can
use IEBCOPY (chapter 5) to delete or rename members of partitioned
data sets, and you can use IEFBR14 (chapter 12) to scratch, catalog,
or uncatalog data sets. However, IEHPROGM has several advantages
over these programs. IEBCOPY scratches or renames members by
copying the entire PDS; IEHPROGM only updates the directory. And
you can encounter problems if you try to scratch, catalog, or
uncatalog a file using IEFBR14. (These problems are discussed in
chapter 12). In short, you should use IEHPROGM rather than the
other utilities for these functions because it is more efficient and
easier to use.

One point that often confuses people is the relationship between
the volumes defined by the DD statements and the volumes referred
to in the control statements. The requirements are really quite simple.
If the system catalog is modified (by a CATLG, UNCATLG, or BLDG
statement), you must include a DD statement to define the catalog
volume. If the catalog itself is not modified, this DD statement may be
omitted. Likewise, a DD statement for the volume containing a file

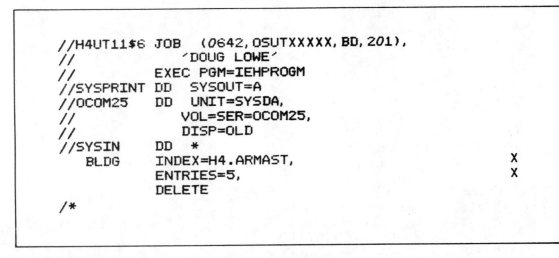

```
//H4UT11$6 JOB   (0642,OSUTXXXXX,BD,201),
//              'DOUG LOWE'
//              EXEC PGM=IEHPROGM
//SYSPRINT DD  SYSOUT=A
//OCOM25    DD  UNIT=SYSDA,
//              VOL=SER=OCOM25,
//              DISP=OLD
//SYSIN    DD  *
   BLDG     INDEX=H4.ARMAST,                          X
            ENTRIES=5,                                X
            DELETE
/*
```

Figure 11-6   Building a generation index using IEHPROGM

referred to by a DSNAME parameter in a control statement is
required only if the VTOC on that volume is modified by a SCRATCH
or RENAME statement.

Objective

Given a problem involving the catalog maintenance functions
described in this chapter, code an acceptable IEHPROGM job.

12

The IEFBR14 Program

In chapter 11, I showed you how to use the IEHPROGM utility to perform various system functions, such as scratching, renaming, cataloging, and uncataloging data sets, and building generation data groups. Many of these functions can be done more easily using an IBM program called IEFBR14. Specifically, IEFBR14 can be used to:

- scratch a data set
- catalog or uncatalog a data set
- create a null (empty) file

Although IBM doesn't consider IEFBR14 to be a utility program (it's not covered in the IBM utilities manual), it is used like one. That's why I'm covering it here.

IEFBR14 is an unusual program in that it doesn't do anything. In fact, its name is derived from an assembler language instruction that causes a return to the program that called it—a BR (branch) to register 14, which always contains the address to return to after a call. If IEFBR14 doesn't do anything, why is it used? Because it allows OS to process the DISP parameter on all the DD statements included in the IEFBR14 step. In other words, even though the files aren't processed by the IEFBR14 program, the operating system deletes the file, keeps it, catalogs it, or uncatalogs it according to what is specified in the DISP parameter of the DD statement for that file.

Because IEFBR14 uses no input or output, I have not included a figure in this chapter to describe the JCL requirements. To execute the program, you specify PGM = IEFBR14 in the EXEC statement. Then, you include a DD statement for each file you want to process, including the appropriate DISP parameter.

IEFBR14 EXAMPLES

As I have already stated, IEFBR14 is used primarily to process the disposition of a file. So I have included an example of a job step that does just that. In addition, IEFBR14 is often used to aid the testing of complicated JCL procedures. I have also included an example of this usage.

Example 1: Processing file dispositions

Figure 12-1 shows how IEFBR14 is used to process the dispositions of four files. Because the DISP parameter for the file named H4.DTRAN4 specifies DELETE, that file will be deleted (scratched) when this step is executed. Similarly, H4.DMA4 will be cataloged,

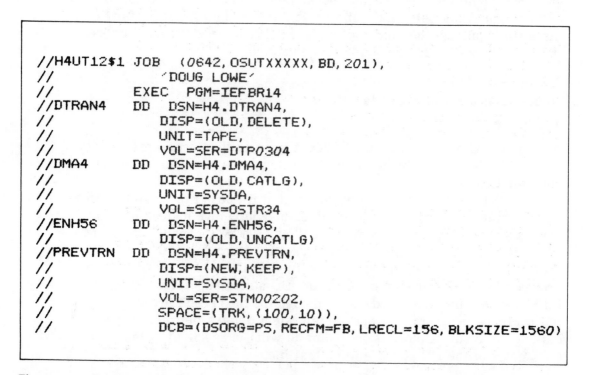

```
//H4UT12$1 JOB   (0642, OSUTXXXXX, BD, 201),
//              'DOUG LOWE'
//           EXEC  PGM=IEFBR14
//DTRAN4    DD   DSN=H4.DTRAN4,
//              DISP=(OLD, DELETE),
//              UNIT=TAPE,
//              VOL=SER=DTP0304
//DMA4      DD   DSN=H4.DMA4,
//              DISP=(OLD, CATLG),
//              UNIT=SYSDA,
//              VOL=SER=OSTR34
//ENH56     DD   DSN=H4.ENH56,
//              DISP=(OLD, UNCATLG)
//PREVTRN   DD   DSN=H4.PREVTRN,
//              DISP=(NEW, KEEP),
//              UNIT=SYSDA,
//              VOL=SER=STM00202,
//              SPACE=(TRK, (100, 10)),
//              DCB=(DSORG=PS, RECFM=FB, LRECL=156, BLKSIZE=1560)
```

Figure 12-1 Processing file dispositions using IEFBR14

and H4.ENH56 will be uncataloged. Finally, a new file named H4.PREVTRN, containing no data, will be created.

Since IEFBR14 is easier to use than IEHPROGM, many programmers use this do-nothing program instead. However, there is a disadvantage to using IEFBR14: If an error occurs when processing a file, subsequent DD statements in the job step won't be processed. For example, in figure 12-1, if the file named H4.DTRAN4 doesn't exist, none of the other files will be processed because of the error. On the other hand, if IEHPROGM is used, this type of error is processed by the utility, and the other control statements are still processed. So although IEHPROGM is more difficult to use than IEFBR14, it is safer.

Example 2: Testing JCL

IEFBR14 can also be used as a dummy program for testing complicated JCL procedures. Since the program can't fail, it always issues a return code of zero and never causes a job to be halted unless there is a JCL error. So processing file dispositions is accomplished just as if the program were real.

To illustrate, look at figure 12-2. It shows a job in three phases of testing. In the first phase, all three steps execute the IEFBR14 program to test the JCL for syntax errors. The DD statements specify dummy file names, so no real data is affected. In the second phase, the IEFBR14 programs are replaced by the real programs, and STEPLIB DD statements are added. These replacements could also be done one at a time to test the system in a modular fashion. In the third phase, the dummy file names are replaced with the real file names, so the programs process the actual data. This results in an orderly, controlled method of testing large job streams.

DISCUSSION

In this chapter, I have shown you how to use the IEFBR14 program for two purposes: (1) to do file manipulation by processing the DISP parameter on DD statements, and (2) to help you test complicated job streams by using it as a dummy program in place of real programs. I hope you now appreciate the value of this do-nothing program.

Objective

Given a problem that requires scratching, cataloging, or uncataloging a data set, or creating an empty data set, code an acceptable job using IEFBR14.

Phase 1

```
//H4DM1200 JOB   (0642,DMTEST1XX,DM,222),
//               'DOUG LOWE'
//CAPSTEP  EXEC  PGM=IEFBR14
//CAPIN    DD   DUMMY
//CAPOUT   DD   DSN=H4.CAPPRL,
//              DISP=(NEW,CATLG),
//              UNIT=SYSDA,
//              VOL=SER=OSTR47,
//              SPACE=(TRK,(10,2),RLSE),
//              DCB=(LRECL=90,BLKSIZE=1800,RECFM=FB)
//PRTSTEP  EXEC  PGM=IEFBR14
//CAPDATA  DD   DSN=H4.CAPPRL,
//              DISP=OLD
//PRTLST   DD   SYSOUT=A
//STMTSTEP EXEC  PGM=IEFBR14
//STMTMAST DD   DUMMY
//CAPDATA  DD   DSN=H4.CAPPRL,
//              DISP=OLD
//STMTLST  DD   SYSOUT=A
//
```

Phase 2

```
//H4DM1200 JOB   (0642,DMTEST2XX,DM,222),
//               'DOUG LOWE'
//CAPSTEP  EXEC  PGM=CAPPROM
//STEPLIB  DD   DSN=H4.USERLIB,
//              DISP=SHR
//CAPIN    DD   DUMMY
//CAPOUT   DD   DSN=H4.CAPPRL,
//              DISP=(NEW,CATLG),
//              UNIT=SYSDA,
//              VOL=SER=OSTR47,
//              SPACE=(TRK,(10,2),RLSE),
//              DCB=(LRECL=90,BLKSIZE=1800,RECFM=FB)
//PRTSTEP  EXEC  PGM=CAPPRT1
//STEPLIB  DD   DSN=H4.USERLIB,
//              DISP=SHR
//CAPDATA  DD   DSN=H4.CAPPRL,
//              DISP=OLD
//PRTLST   DD   SYSOUT=A
//STMTSTEP EXEC  PGM=CAPPRT2
//STEPLIB  DD   DSN=H4.USERLIB,
//              DISP=SHR
//STMTMAST DD   DUMMY
//CAPDATA  DD   DSN=H4.CAPPRL,
//              DISP=OLD
//STMTLST  DD   SYSOUT=A
//
```

Figure 12-2   Testing a job stream in three phases using IEFBR14 (part 1 of 2)

```
Phase 3

//H4DM1200 JOB   (0642,DMPRODXXX,DM,222),
//               'DOUG LOWE'
//CAPSTEP  EXEC  PGM=CAPPROM
//STEPLIB  DD   DSN=H4.USERLIB,
//              DISP=SHR
//CAPIN    DD   DSN=H4.CAPMAST,
//              DISP=OLD
//CAPOUT   DD   DSN=H4.CAPPRL,
//              DISP=(NEW,CATLG),
//              UNIT=SYSDA,
//              VOL=SER=OSTR47,
//              SPACE=(TRK,(10,2),RLSE),
//              DCB=(LRECL=90,BLKSIZE=1800,RECFM=FB)
//PRTSTEP  EXEC  PGM=CAPPRT1
//STEPLIB  DD   DSN=H4.USERLIB,
//              DISP=SHR
//CAPDATA  DD   DSN=H4.CAPPRL,
//              DISP=OLD
//PRTLST   DD   SYSOUT=A
//STMTSTEP EXEC  PGM=CAPPRT2
//STEPLIB  DD   DSN=H4.USERLIB,
//              DISP=SHR
//STMTMAST DD   DSN=H4.STMTMAST,
//              DISP=OLD
//CAPDATA  DD   DSN=H4.CAPPRL,
//              DISP=OLD
//STMTLST  DD   SYSOUT=A
//
```

Figure 12-2 Testing a job stream in three phases using IEFBR14 (part 2 of 2)

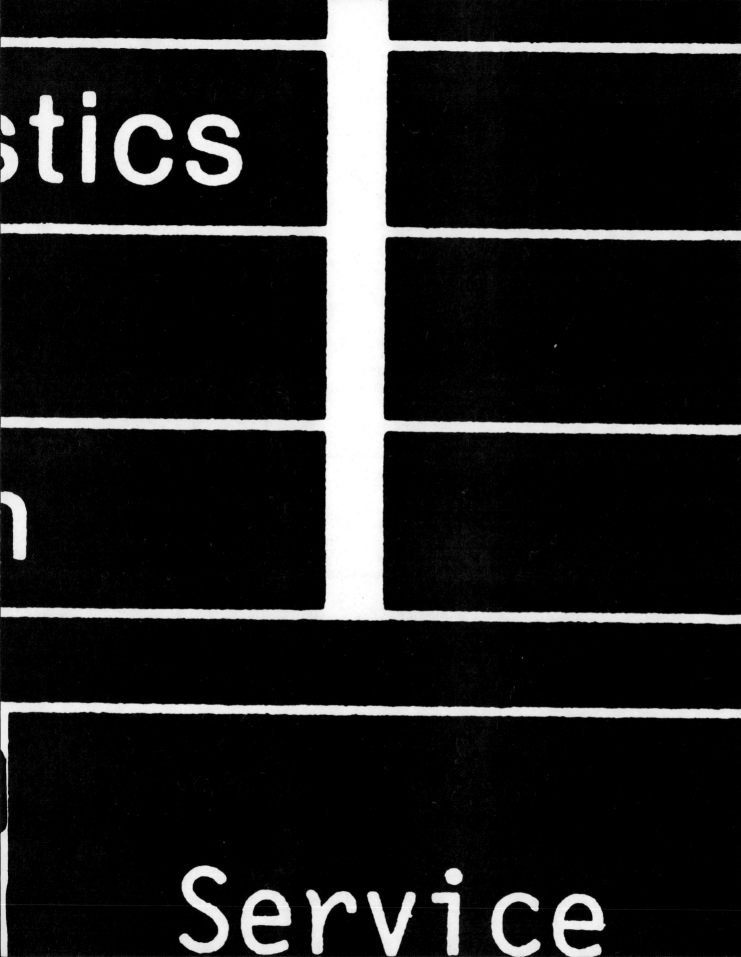

13

The Sort/Merge Program

Since input data seldom enters a computer system in the order of the desired output, the sort/merge program is frequently used. As a result, most computers provide sort/merge programs that are generalized so you can customize the sorting and merging to fit your specific file requirements. You provide control information, and the sort/merge adjusts itself accordingly to sort or merge the records in the sequence you specify.

There are two functions of the sort/merge program (as the name implies). You can use it to:

- *sort* records into a specified sequence
- *merge* records (already in sequence) from multiple files into one file

When you request the sort function, both the sort and merge may be executed, depending on the number of records in the file to be sorted. When you request the merge function, only the merge will be executed.

IBM provides the user with one of three versions of its sort/merge program, depending on the hardware installed on the system. In addition, there are software vendors who will sell you still other versions. In this chapter, I'll only discuss the JCL and sort/merge control statements for the IBM-supplied versions. However, please bear in mind that you only have to make minor changes in the JCL when you change from an IBM sort/merge to another vendor's sort/merge package. You should check with your installation for more specific guidelines regarding the sort/merge program.

EXECUTING THE SORT/MERGE PROGRAM THROUGH JCL

The sort/merge program can be executed in one of two ways: either through JCL statements like the other utilities or through linkages to user-written programs in languages like COBOL, PL/I, and assembler. I'll get to the JCL for executing sorts from user-written programs in a few minutes. First, however, I want to show you how to execute the sort/merge program on its own.

JCL requirements

Figure 13-1 shows the JCL statements required to execute the sort/merge program. As you can see, this JCL is somewhat different than that used to execute the other utility programs. To begin with, the name of the sort/merge program varies from one system to another, so you should check with your installation to determine the program name to specify on the EXEC statement. In addition, a PARM parameter is coded on the EXEC statement. I'll explain the values that can be coded in the PARM parameter in just a moment.

The SORTLIB DD statement defines the library where the support modules for the sort/merge program reside. Usually, the name of this library is SYS1.SORTLIB, but it may be different at your installation. SYSOUT defines the listing produced by the sort/merge program. It is usually coded SYSOUT = A. Notice that the sort/merge program uses the DD name SYSOUT for the message listing, while the other utilities use SYSPRINT.

```
//stepname EXEC  PGM=sort-program-name (usually SORT)
//SORTLIB   DD   sort program library (usually SYS1.SORTLIB)
//SYSOUT    DD   message listing (SYSOUT=A)
//SORTIN    DD   input file for sort operations
//SORTINnn  DD   input files for merge operations
//SORTOUT   DD   output file
//SORTWKnn  DD   work files
//SYSIN     DD   control file (*)
     control statements
/*
```

Figure 13-1   JCL requirements for the sort/merge program

SORTIN defines the input file to be sorted. If you are requesting a merge operation, you use SORTIN01, SORTIN02, etc., to define the two or more files to be merged. If you are sorting more than one file, you can concatenate them to the SORTIN file like this:

```
//SORTIN    DD   DSN=INFILE1,
//               DISP=OLD
//         DD   DSN=INFILE2,
//               DISP=OLD
```

In this case, the sort program will treat INFILE1 and INFILE2 as a single file to be sorted.

SORTOUT defines the output file where the sorted records are written. It can be a new file with DISP = (NEW,KEEP) or (NEW,CATLG), or it can be an extension of an old file with DISP = (MOD,KEEP).

SORTWKnn DD statements are work areas defined on tape or direct-access volumes. The nn may be a number from 01 to 32 for tape SORTWKs or 01 to 06 for direct-access SORTWKs. Actually, tape SORTWKs are rare, so you'll usually find three to six direct-access SORTWK areas defined. A merge-only function doesn't require work areas, so you can omit the SORTWKs from the JCL for a merge operation.

The amount of space you request for these intermediate storage areas is determined by record length, the number of records to be sorted, and the number of intermediate areas you define. Formulas for calculating intermediate storage requirements differ depending on the version of the sort/merge and the type of hardware installed. You should check with your installation to find how to calculate the most efficient size for these work areas on your system. And it's a good idea to use the CONTIG option in the SPACE parameter for these areas.

SYSIN defines the input control statements for the sort/merge program. It can define instream data by coding DD *, or it can have a DSN that specifies a separate file or member of a partitoned data set that contains the sort/merge control statements.

Coding PARM values for the sort/merge   You can supply five PARM parameter options to the sort/merge in a positional list, as shown in figure 13-2. Here is a description of each, along with recommendations on using them:

1. Coding the first subparameter, which changes the sort technique, is not recommended because the sort/merge will derive an

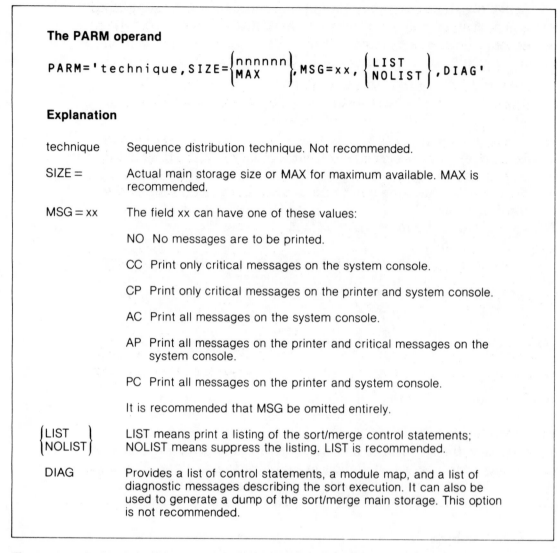

The PARM operand

PARM='technique,SIZE=$\begin{Bmatrix} nnnnnn \\ MAX \end{Bmatrix}$,MSG=xx, $\begin{Bmatrix} LIST \\ NOLIST \end{Bmatrix}$,DIAG'

Explanation

technique   Sequence distribution technique. Not recommended.

SIZE =   Actual main storage size or MAX for maximum available. MAX is recommended.

MSG = xx   The field xx can have one of these values:

    NO No messages are to be printed.

    CC Print only critical messages on the system console.

    CP Print only critical messages on the printer and system console.

    AC Print all messages on the system console.

    AP Print all messages on the printer and critical messages on the system console.

    PC Print all messages on the printer and system console.

    It is recommended that MSG be omitted entirely.

$\begin{Bmatrix} LIST \\ NOLIST \end{Bmatrix}$ LIST means print a listing of the sort/merge control statements; NOLIST means suppress the listing. LIST is recommended.

DIAG   Provides a list of control statements, a module map, and a list of diagnostic messages describing the sort execution. It can also be used to generate a dump of the sort/merge main storage. This option is not recommended.

Figure 13-2   PARM values for the sort/merge EXEC statement

appropriate technique by itself. It's mentioned here since it is positional, so you must code a comma to indicate its absence.

2. You can specify the amount of main storage to be allocated to the program by coding SIZE = core-size or SIZE = MAX. If you code SIZE = MAX, the program will calculate the available main storage and allocate it, resulting in a more efficient sort operation. I recommend that you always code SIZE = MAX.

3. You can override the options specified at your installation concerning the printing of messages by coding MSG = xx, where xx is

one of the two-character codes listed in figure 13-2. I recommend that you don't override the options specified by your installation. So don't code this option.

4. The listing option can be overridden by coding either LIST or NOLIST. LIST causes all program control statements to be printed; NOLIST suppresses all printing. I recommend that you code LIST if LIST isn't your installation default.

5. The fifth option, DIAG, should never be used unless you need a detail listing of the modules of the sort/merge program. The only time you should select this option is when the sort/merge program doesn't work properly and you are reporting that to IBM or the software vendor.

Figure 13-3 gives three examples of PARM parameters. The PARM in example 1 specifies that 100,000 bytes of main storage should be used for the sort/merge program and that no messages or sort/merge control statements should be printed. In example 2, the PARM says to use as much main storage as is available for the sort/merge run, to print critical mesages on both the printer and system console, and to print a listing of the sort/merge control statements. And in example 3, the PARM simply says to use as much main storage as possible for the program. I recommend that you code all sort/merge PARMs like example 3.

Sort/merge control statements

The sort/merge program uses one main control statement: the SORT/MERGE statement, illustrated in figure 13-4. Although there are

```
Example 1

//EX1        EXEC  PGM=SORT,
//                 PARM=',SIZE=100000,MSG=NO,NOLIST'

Example 2

//EX2        EXEC  PGM=SORT,
//                 PARM=',SIZE=MAX,MSG=CP,LIST'

Example 3

//EX3        EXEC  PGM=SORT,
//                 PARM=',SIZE=MAX'
```

Figure 13-3 Examples of PARM values for the sort/merge program

---

The SORT/MERGE statement

Format 1

```
{SORT }  FIELDS=(location,length,sequence,...),
{MERGE}  FORMAT=format
```

Format 2

```
{SORT }
{MERGE}  FIELDS=(location,length,format,sequence,...)
```

Explanation

SORT   Specifies a sort operation.

MERGE   Specifies a merge operation.

FIELDS   Specifies the keys used for sorting or merging. The values that may
            be coded are:

            location   The beginning position of the key within the record.

            length   The length of the key field.

            format   The data format. Code CH for character data, BI for
                       binary data, PD for packed decimal data, or ZD for
                       zoned decimal data. Code format in FIELDS parameter
                       only if format 2 is used.

            sequence   The sorting sequence—A for ascending, D for
                       descending.

FORMAT   The format of the key data—used only in format 1. Code CH for
            character data, BI for binary data, PD for packed decimal data, or
            ZD for zoned decimal data.

Note: Position one of the SORT/MERGE statement must be blank.

Figure 13-4   The SORT/MERGE Statement

other sort/merge control statements, most of them aren't used very
often, so I haven't covered them here. The one exception is the
RECORD statement, which is required to execute the SORT/MERGE
program from certain user programs. I'll get to it in a few minutes.

The SORT/MERGE statement is used to initiate a sort or merge
operation. The IBM sort/merge manual treats SORT and MERGE as
two separate statements, but I have combined them here because
their formats are identical. The SORT/MERGE statement has two
parameters: FIELDS and FORMAT. Notice that in the second format

shown for the SORT/MERGE statement, the information supplied by the FORMAT parameter is supplied instead in the FIELDS parameter.

The purpose of the FIELDS parameter in the SORT/MERGE control statement is to tell the sort/merge program the sequence you want the output to be in. Each series of location, length, and sequence subparameters makes up a single *key field* by which the output is to be sequenced. Then, the key fields specified in the control statement make up a *control word*. Internally, the sort/merge program views the control word as a single field and uses it to control the sequencing of the file.

To illustrate, look at figure 13-5. It shows ten unsorted records, the SORT control statement to sort those records into the desired sequence, and the result of the operation: the sorted records.

In this example, the file is to be sorted by a control word made up of three key fields. According to the FIELDS parameter of this SORT control statement, the program is directed to (1) sort the records in ascending order according to the 6-character field that begins in position 3 of each record; (2) within that sequence, sort the records into descending order according to the 3-character field that begins in position 11; and (3) within that sequence, sort the records into ascending order according to the 3-character field that begins in position 18. In other words, the subfields of the SORT control statement indicate major to minor sequencing from left to right in the control statement.

You can see the result of this sequencing in the bottom part of figure 13-5. The records are sorted into ascending sequence according to the values in positions 3-8. The records that have the same data in this field (012345 and 019412) are sorted into descending sequence according to the values in positions 11-13. Finally, the records that still have the same value (019412 in the first field and 605 in the second field) are sorted into ascending sequence according to the values found in positions 18-20.

The FORMAT parameter of the SORT/MERGE control statement indicates what type of data is contained in the key fields. In this case, it's character (CH) data. You can also code BI for binary data, PD for packed decimal data, or ZD for zoned decimal data. If the fields contain different types of data, you use the second SORT statement format in figure 13-4. For example, the SORT statement that follows would perform the same sequencing as that shown in figure 13-5 if the fields were different data types:

```
SORT FIELDS=(3,6,CH,A,11,3,BI,D,18,3,ZD,A)
```

This assumes that the first field is character data, the second is binary, and the third is zoned decimal.

Unsorted records

Position:	3-8	11-13	18-20
	012345	AAA	012
	012345	ABC	907
	011947	RB2	106
	047693	AAT	999
	142342	BBR	212
	002973	972	660
	112233	617	127
	019412	322	432
	019412	605	692
	019412	605	000

SORT statement

```
SORT      FIELDS=(3,6,A,11,3,D,18,3,A),FORMAT=CH
```

Sorted records

Position:	3-8	11-13	18-20
	002973	972	660
	011947	RB2	106
	012345	ABC	907
	012345	AAA	012
	019412	605	000
	019412	605	692
	019412	322	432
	047693	AAT	999
	112233	617	127
	142342	BBR	212

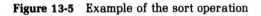

Figure 13-5 Example of the sort operation

To illustrate the use of the MERGE statement, look at figure 13-6. It shows two files, already in the desired sequence, that I want to merge into a single sequenced file. After the MERGE statement is executed, the output is in the same sequence as the input, but the two

	Input file 1		**Input file 2**	
Position:	1-5	9	1-5	9
	01234	A	01234	B
	02694	A	01234	E
	02694	D	02988	A
	02988	R	06611	T
	05617	B	07122	R
	05617	C	88216	A
	98999	D	98999	A
	98999	E	98999	Z
	99999	Z	99999	T

MERGE statement

```
MERGE    FIELDS=(1,5,A,9,1,A),FORMAT=CH
```

Merged file

Position:	1-5	9
	01234	A
	01234	B
	01234	E
	02694	A
	02694	D
	02988	A
	02988	R
	05617	B
	05617	C
	06611	T
	07122	R
	88216	A
	98999	A
	98999	D
	98999	E
	98999	Z
	99999	T
	99999	Z

Figure 13-6   Example of the merge operation

files are combined into one sequenced file. The subfields of the
MERGE statement comprise the control word for the merge operation
that is similar to that for the sort operation, and the same rules
apply.

Sample jobs

Figure 13-7 shows a job to execute a sort operation. It sorts a file
named H4.TEMPCOST into the sequence specified in the SORT statement, using SORTWK01 through SORTWK03 for intermediate work
areas, then writes the sorted output onto the file defined by
SORTOUT (H4.SORTCOST).

Figure 13-8 shows a job to execute a merge operation that reads
three SORTIN files and merges them into one output file,
H4.HISTALL. Remember that the three input files are already in the
sequence defined by the MERGE statement, and they will now be combined into one output file in that same sequence.

```
//H4UT13$7 JOB   (0642,OSUTXXXXX,BD,201),
//               'DOUG LOWE'
//SORTSTEP EXEC  PGM=SORT,
//               PARM=',SIZE=MAX'
//SORTLIB   DD   DSN=SYS1.SORTLIB,
//               DISP=SHR
//SYSOUT    DD   SYSOUT=A
//SORTIN    DD   DSN=H4.TEMPCOST,
//               DISP=OLD
//SORTWK01  DD   UNIT=SYSDA,
//               SPACE=(CYL,10,,CONTIG)
//SORTWK02  DD   UNIT=SYSDA,
//               SPACE=(CYL,10,,CONTIG)
//SORTWK03  DD   UNIT=SYSDA,
//               SPACE=(CYL,10,,CONTIG)
//SORTOUT   DD   DSN=H4.SORTCOST,
//               DISP=(NEW,CATLG),
//               UNIT=3350,
//               VOL=SER=OSTR22,
//               SPACE=(CYL,(20,10),RLSE),
//               DCB=(RECFM=FB,LRECL=65,BLKSIZE=3250)
//SYSIN     DD   *
  SORT        FIELDS=(1,7,A,21,1,A,37,6,D),FORMAT=CH
/*
```

Figure 13-7 Sorting a file

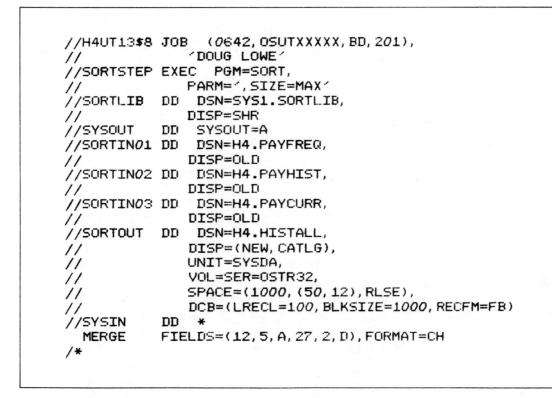

```
//H4UT13$8 JOB   (0642,OSUTXXXXX,BD,201),
//               'DOUG LOWE'
//SORTSTEP EXEC  PGM=SORT,
//               PARM=',SIZE=MAX'
//SORTLIB  DD   DSN=SYS1.SORTLIB,
//               DISP=SHR
//SYSOUT   DD   SYSOUT=A
//SORTIN01 DD   DSN=H4.PAYFREQ,
//               DISP=OLD
//SORTIN02 DD   DSN=H4.PAYHIST,
//               DISP=OLD
//SORTIN03 DD   DSN=H4.PAYCURR,
//               DISP=OLD
//SORTOUT  DD   DSN=H4.HISTALL,
//               DISP=(NEW,CATLG),
//               UNIT=SYSDA,
//               VOL=SER=OSTR32,
//               SPACE=(1000,(50,12),RLSE),
//               DCB=(LRECL=100,BLKSIZE=1000,RECFM=FB)
//SYSIN    DD   *
   MERGE      FIELDS=(12,5,A,27,2,D),FORMAT=CH
/*
```

Figure 13-8   Merging three files

EXECUTING THE SORT/MERGE PROGRAM FROM A USER-WRITTEN PROGRAM

For certain applications, you may find it more convenient to code a *COBOL sort*, *PL/I sort*, or *assembler sort* instead of a *standalone sort* (one executed through JCL). That means the sort/merge program is executed because of special statements you've put in your program.

The RECORD statement, illustrated in figure 13-9, is required when the sort/merge program is called from a PL/I or assembler-language program. As you can see, the RECORD statement has two parameters. TYPE specifies the record type as fixed (F) or variable (V). LENGTH specifies the length of each record. Note that the record length must be enclosed in parentheses. To illustrate the use of the RECORD statement, consider this example from a PL/I program:

```
CALL PLISRTA (' SORT FIELDS=(1,80,CH,A)',
              ' RECORD TYPE=F,LENGTH=(80) ',
              60000,
              RETCODE);
```

The RECORD statement

```
RECORD TYPE=type,
       LENGTH=(length)
```

Explanation

TYPE   Type of records. Code F for fixed length, V for variable length.

LENGTH   Length of records. Be sure to use parentheses.

Figure 13-9   The RECORD statement

Here, the RECORD statement specifies fixed length records that are 80 bytes long. (The two parameters following the RECORD statement specify the number of bytes of main storage available to the sort and the name of the variable that will receive the sort return code.)

Figure 13-10 shows the JCL to execute a sort from a program written in COBOL, PL/I, or assembler language. The program specified in the EXEC statement is the name of the user-written program. The DD statements are the same as if there were no sort involved, except for the SORTWK DD statements and the SORTLIB DD statement. These are coded the same as for standalone sorts. The source program specifies which of the other files is to be sorted and which is to hold the sorted records. No control statements are used because the source program gives the sort/merge specifications. Consult the programmer's guide for your language to find out how to execute the sort/merge from your own programs.

DISCUSSION

In this chapter, I've presented a general view of the IBM sort/merge programs by showing the JCL and sort/merge control statements necessary to execute any version now in use. However, as I mentioned at the beginning of this chapter, there are three currently supported versions of the IBM-supplied sort/merge program and at least one major non-IBM sort/merge package available for use on the System/360-370. (The non-IBM package I'm referring to is Whitlow Computer Systems' SYNCSORT.) As a result, some of the information presented here may not be required by the version of the sort/merge installed on your computer system, or there may be ways to increase the efficiency of the sorting and merging operation by coding the JCL in a different way than shown here. So I recommend that you study

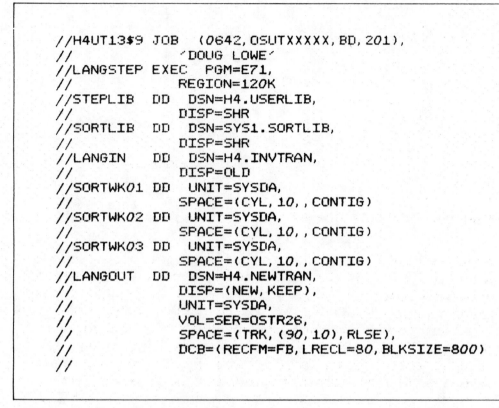

```
//H4UT13$9 JOB  (0642,OSUTXXXXX,BD,201),
//              'DOUG LOWE'
//LANGSTEP EXEC  PGM=E71,
//              REGION=120K
//STEPLIB  DD   DSN=H4.USERLIB,
//              DISP=SHR
//SORTLIB  DD   DSN=SYS1.SORTLIB,
//              DISP=SHR
//LANGIN   DD   DSN=H4.INVTRAN,
//              DISP=OLD
//SORTWK01 DD   UNIT=SYSDA,
//              SPACE=(CYL,10,,CONTIG)
//SORTWK02 DD   UNIT=SYSDA,
//              SPACE=(CYL,10,,CONTIG)
//SORTWK03 DD   UNIT=SYSDA,
//              SPACE=(CYL,10,,CONTIG)
//LANGOUT  DD   DSN=H4.NEWTRAN,
//              DISP=(NEW,KEEP),
//              UNIT=SYSDA,
//              VOL=SER=OSTR26,
//              SPACE=(TRK,(90,10),RLSE),
//              DCB=(RECFM=FB,LRECL=80,BLKSIZE=800)
//
```

Figure 13-10   Executing a COBOL, PL/I, or assembler sort

the sort/merge standards in use at your installation and pattern your sort/merge JCL and control statements after them. Then, with experience, you'll be able to code effecient sort/merge jobs.

Terminology

sort	COBOL sort
merge	PL/I sort
key field	assembler sort
control word	standalone sort

Objective

Given reference material, write the JCL and sort/merge control statements to execute the IBM-supplied OS sort/merge program for given specifications.

sting:

VERSION 1 RELEA

ATTRIBUTES(FULL)
CHARSET(60,EBCDIC
NOCOMPILE(S)
FLAG(I)
LINECOUNT(55)
MARGINS(2,72,0)

14

IDCAMS:
The Access-Methods-Services
Program

In this chapter, I'm going to show you how to use the VSAM utility program, IDCAMS. Because of the complexity of IDCAMS, this chapter is divided into four topics. Topic 1 will provide the background information required for you to use IDCAMS. Topic 2 will show you how to use IDCAMS to set up the disk areas required by VSAM files. Topic 3 shows you how to copy or print the contents of VSAM files. Topic 4 covers some of the VSAM catalog maintenance functions available with IDCAMS. Topics 2, 3, and 4 are independent. So, after you've read topic 1, you may read the other three topics in any order you wish.

TOPIC 1   Using IDCAMS

1

IDCAMS is the main utility program for processing VSAM files. It is called the *Access-Methods-Services program* because it can perform a variety of utility services using several different access methods. Unlike the other OS utilities, IDCAMS can process sequential files, ISAM files, or VSAM files (entry-sequenced, key-sequenced, or numbered). The only file organization IDCAMS can't process is partitioned.

For VSAM files, you can use IDCAMS to:

- define a VSAM master or user catalog
- define a VSAM data space
- define a VSAM cluster
- load a VSAM file from a non-VSAM file
- copy a VSAM file
- print a VSAM file
- list the entries of a VSAM catalog
- scratch (delete) a VSAM file

In other words, IDCAMS does for VSAM files what IEBGENER, IEBPTPCH, IEBISAM, IEHLIST, and IEHPROGM do for non-VSAM files.

For non-VSAM files, IDCAMS can perform several basic functions. For instance, you can use IDCAMS to:

- copy a non-VSAM file
- print a non-VSAM file
- catalog a non-VSAM file in a VSAM catalog
- scratch a non-VSAM file cataloged in a VSAM catalog

So, IDCAMS can be used instead of the other utility programs for many basic utility functions.

In this topic, I'm going to show you the basics of using IDCAMS. Then, in the next three topics, I'll show you how to perform specific utility functions using IDCAMS.

JCL REQUIREMENTS

Figure 14-1 illustrates the basic job-control statements needed to execute the IDCAMS program. Like the other utility programs, SYSPRINT and SYSIN are used to define the message listing and the control file. You may use any ddnames you wish to define the input and output files—control statements will specify which files are input and which are output.

The STEPCAT DD statement is used only if you wish to use a user catalog. If coded, it must be the first statement after the EXEC statement (or STEPLIB, if used). The STEPCAT DD statement simply identifies the catalog to be used for that job step. If you wish to specify a user catalog that is to be used for all of the steps in a job, you can use a JOBCAT DD statement instead. The JOBCAT statement is coded in the same way as STEPCAT, except that it appears

```
//stepname EXEC  PGM=IDCAMS
//STEPCAT  DD   step catalog (not always required)
//SYSPRINT DD   message listing (SYSOUT=A)
//ddname   DD   input or output file
//SYSIN    DD   control file (*)
      control statements
/*
```

Note: Instead of a STEPCAT DD statement, a JOBCAT DD statement may
be placed immediately after the JOB statement. STEPCAT or
JOBCAT is used only if you wish to override the master catalog.

Figure 14-1 JCL requirements for the IDCAMS utility

immediately after the JOB statement. In the topics that follow, you
will see how the JOBCAT and STEPCAT DD statements are used.

CONTROL STATEMENTS

Like the other utility programs, IDCAMS requires control statements.
However, because IDCAMS was developed separately from the other
utility programs, its control statements are coded differently. Here's a
summary of the differences:

1. A space or a comma can be used to separate the parameters.

2. Instead of an equals sign to indicate a parameter's value, each
    parameter name is immediately followed by its value enclosed in
    parentheses. Here's an example:

    ```
    NAME(MMACAT)
    ```

3. To continue a statement on the next line, code a hyphen (-) after a
    parameter and continue the next parameter or function on the
    next line. The hyphen may be preceded by a space for readabili-
    ty. Here's an example:

    ```
    FILE(LIBAREA) -
    VOLUME(USER20)
    ```

    Although the IBM manual documents 23 IDCAMS control
statements with literally hundreds of possible operands, I'm only
going to cover eight in this chapter. Their functions are summarized
in figure 14-2 for your reference. These statements are all you'll need

Control statement	Function	Topic
DEFINE USERCATALOG	Define a user catalog	2
DEFINE SPACE	Define a data space	2
DEFINE CLUSTER	Define a cluster	2
DEFINE NONVSAM	Catalog a non-VSAM file	4
REPRO	Copy or load a file	3
PRINT	Print a file	3
DELETE	Scratch a file	4
LISTCAT	List catalog entries	4
ALTER	Modify catalog entries	4

Figure 14-2   The IDCAMS control statements covered in this chapter

to perform most of the functions for which you'll use IDCAMS. The other IDCAMS statements are infrequently used.

DISCUSSION

If you feel confused about the IDCAMS utility, relax. At this point, I only expect you to know three things: (1) the JCL statements required to execute IDCAMS, (2) the rules for coding control statements, and (3) the correct control statement to use for each IDCAMS function. I don't expect you to be able to use IDCAMS yet.

In the next three topics, I'll show you how to use IDCAMS for a variety of utility functions. Topic 2 covers the DEFINE statement, used to define VSAM areas. Topic 3 covers the REPRO and PRINT statements, used to copy and print data sets. Topic 4 covers the DELETE, LISTCAT, and ALTER statements, used to maintain VSAM catalogs. These topics are independent, so feel free to study them in any order you wish.

Objectives

1. List the JCL statements required to execute IDCAMS.
2. List the rules for creating IDCAMS control statements.
3. List the names and functions of the IDCAMS control statements.

TOPIC 2   Defining VSAM Areas With IDCAMS

2

Before you can process a VSAM file, you must do three things. First, you must create a catalog to record the characteristics of the file. Second, you must create a *data space* that will contain the file. Third, you must create the VSAM file itself, called a *cluster*.

In VSAM, there are two types of catalogs. The *master catalog* is the main catalog for a VSAM system. The master catalog contains entries for data sets and other catalogs, called *user catalogs*. The user catalogs in turn contain entries for other data sets. Figure 14-3 shows the relationships between the master catalog, user catalogs, and individual data sets. Note that a VSAM catalog can contain entries for non-VSAM files as well as VSAM files.

Most installations that use VSAM have master and user catalogs already established, so you will probably never have to define one yourself. As a result, this discussion is presented only as background information so you'll know how it's done. You should find out what catalog you're to use by checking with your computer installation's management.

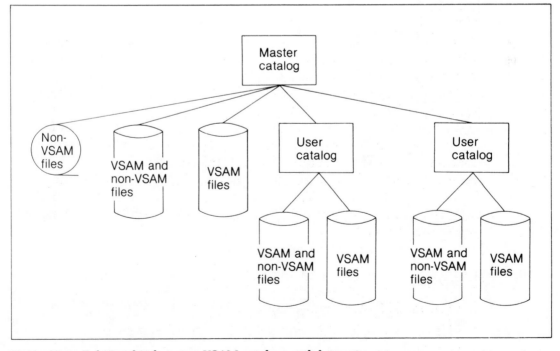

Figure 14-3   Relationship between VSAM catalogs and data sets

Before you can load and use a VSAM file, you have to define a
data space. To do this, you tell OS the volume, device type, and space
requirements of the data set. Then, you must define the cluster (the
data set itself) by specifying the type of VSAM data set, the estimated
number of records, and the attributes of the file. To perform these
functions through IDCAMS, you use the DEFINE statement.

THE DEFINE STATEMENT

The DEFINE statement is the basic IDCAMS statement used for defin-
ing VSAM areas. Three variations of DEFINE are commonly used:
DEFINE USERCATALOG, DEFINE SPACE, and DEFINE CLUSTER.
These are illustrated in figures 14-4, 14-5, and 14-6. DEFINE USER-
CATALOG is used to define a user catalog; DEFINE SPACE is used to
define a data space; and DEFINE CLUSTER is used to define a

The DEFINE USERCATALOG statement

```
DEFINE USERCATALOG -
        (NAME(catalog-name) -
          MASTERPW(password) -
          FILE(ddname) -
          VOLUME(vol-ser) -

         (RECORDS )
         {TRACKS   } (primary secondary))
         (CYLINDERS)
```

Explanation

NAME — The name assigned to the new catalog.

MASTERPW — The password to be associated with this catalog.

FILE — The name of a DD statement that identifies the volume that will contain the catalog.

VOLUME — The volume serial number of the volume to contain the catalog.

{RECORDS TRACKS CYLINDERS} — The space allocation for the catalog. RECORDS, TRACKS, or CYLINDERS specifies the type of space to be allocated. Primary specifies the initial allocation, and secondary specifies the secondary allocation in case the primary space becomes full.

Figure 14-4   The DEFINE USERCATALOG statement

```
The DEFINE SPACE statement

DEFINE SPACE -
         (FILE(ddname) -
           VOLUMES(vol-ser) -

          ⎧RECORDS  ⎫
          ⎨TRACKS   ⎬ (primary secondary) -
          ⎩CYLINDERS⎭

           RECORDSIZE(average maximum)) -

           CATALOG(catalog-name/password)
```

Explanation

FILE	The name of a DD statement that identifies the volume that will contain the data space.
VOLUMES	The volume serial number of the volume that will contain the data space.
⎧RECORDS⎫ ⎨TRACKS⎬ ⎩CYLINDERS⎭	The space allocation for the data space. RECORDS, TRACKS, or CYLINDERS specifies the unit of allocation. Primary specifies how many units to allocate initially, and secondary specifies the secondary allocation in case the primary space becomes full.
RECORDSIZE	The average and maximum record size.
CATALOG	The name and password of the catalog that will contain this entry.

Figure 14-5   The DEFINE SPACE statement

cluster. There are many other variations of the DEFINE statement (for example, DEFINE PATH, DEFINE MASTERCATALOG, or DEFINE ALTERNATEINDEX), but they aren't used very often.

Defining a user catalog

Figure 14-7 shows a job to create a user catalog using IDCAMS. Here, the DEFINE USERCATALOG statement is used. The outer pair of parentheses contains information specifying the catalog's characteristics: the name of the catalog is H4UCAT; the master password is MMA (this password must be specified on any request to access the catalog); the catalog is to reside on the volume defined by the ddname VSAMC1; the volume serial number is VSAMC1; and the number of records (indicating the primary and secondary space allocation for the catalog) is 100 records for the primary allocation and 20 records for secondary allocations. (VSAM will allow up to 15

The DEFINE CLUSTER statement

```
DEFINE CLUSTER -
        (NAME(cluster-name) -
          FILE(ddname) -
          VOLUMES(vol-ser) -

        ⎧RECORDS  ⎫
        ⎨TRACKS   ⎬ (primary secondary) -
        ⎩CYLINDERS⎭

          RECORDSIZE(average maximum) -

        ⎧INDEXED   ⎫
        ⎨NONINDEXED⎬ -
        ⎩NUMBERED  ⎭

          KEYS(length offset)) -
        CATALOG(catalog-name/password)
```

Explanation

NAME	The name assigned to this cluster.
FILE	The name of a DD statement that identifies the volume that will contain the cluster.
VOLUMES	The volume serial number of the volume that will contain this cluster.
⎧RECORDS⎫ ⎨TRACKS⎬ ⎩CYLINDERS⎭	The space allocation for the cluster. RECORDS, TRACKS, or CYLINDERS specifies the unit of allocation. Primary specifies the number of units to be allocated initially, and secondary specifies the secondary allocation in case the primary space becomes full.
RECORDSIZE	The average and maximum record size.
⎧INDEXED⎫ ⎨NONINDEXED⎬ ⎩NUMBERED⎭	The VSAM file organization—INDEXED for key-sequenced files, NONINDEXED for entry-sequenced files, and NUMBERED for numbered files.
KEYS	The length and offset of the keys for INDEXED files.
CATALOG	The name and password of the catalog that will contain this cluster entry.

Figure 14-6   The DEFINE CLUSTER statement

secondary allocations. Once this limit has been reached, you must allocate more space for the catalog.)

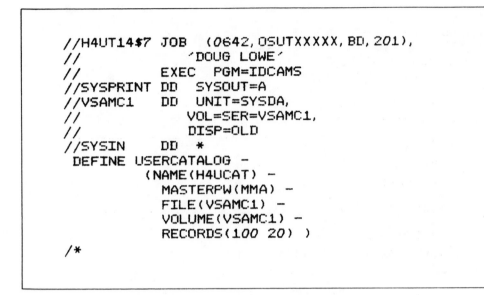

```
//H4UT14$7 JOB   (0642,OSUTXXXXX,BD,201),
//              'DOUG LOWE'
//              EXEC  PGM=IDCAMS
//SYSPRINT DD   SYSOUT=A
//VSAMC1   DD   UNIT=SYSDA,
//              VOL=SER=VSAMC1,
//              DISP=OLD
//SYSIN    DD  *
  DEFINE USERCATALOG -
         (NAME(H4UCAT) -
          MASTERPW(MMA) -
          FILE(VSAMC1) -
          VOLUME(VSAMC1) -
          RECORDS(100 20) )
/*
```

Figure 14-7   Creating a VSAM user catalog using IDCAMS

Defining a data space

Once the user catalog has been established, the next step is to define the area that will hold the VSAM data set. To do this, you must use the DEFINE SPACE command. Figure 14-8 illustrates a job to define a data space on a volume named OSTR21 that uses 20 cylinders of primary space and 5 cylinders for secondary allocations. Again, up to 15 secondary allocations are allowed by VSAM. Notice that this volume is identified in a preceding DD statement. Notice too the use of the keyword VOLUMES, in contrast to VOLUME used for a DEFINE USERCATALOG statement. The data space is to be cataloged in the user catalog I created in the previous example (H4UCAT). The master password, MMA, is provided by the CATALOG function of the DEFINE command. The STEPCAT DD statement identifies the user catalog.

Defining a cluster

As I mentioned, a VSAM data set is called a cluster. After space has been allocated on the direct-access device and an entry is made in the appropriate catalog, you can define a cluster.

Figure 14-9 shows you how to define all three types of VSAM clusters: key-sequenced, entry-sequenced, and numbered. For the entry-sequenced and numbered files, I've shown the DEFINE statements alone; the rest of the job statements will be the same as they are for the key-sequenced file.

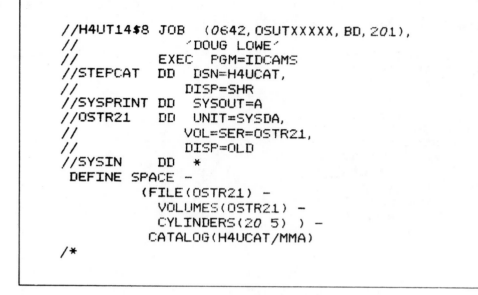

```
//H4UT14$8 JOB  (0642,OSUTXXXXX,BD,201),
//             'DOUG LOWE'
//         EXEC  PGM=IDCAMS
//STEPCAT   DD   DSN=H4UCAT,
//               DISP=SHR
//SYSPRINT DD    SYSOUT=A
//OSTR21    DD   UNIT=SYSDA,
//               VOL=SER=OSTR21,
//               DISP=OLD
//SYSIN     DD   *
 DEFINE SPACE -
        (FILE(OSTR21) -
          VOLUMES(OSTR21) -
          CYLINDERS(20 5)  ) -
        CATALOG(H4UCAT/MMA)
 /*
```

Figure 14-8   Creating a VSAM data space using IDCAMS

In the first set of parentheses, the DEFINE CLUSTER statement
gives the characteristics of the cluster. Then, the CATALOG function
specifies the name of the user catalog defined by the STEPCAT DD
statement. Also provided is the master password (MMA) required to
access the catalog.

In this example, the key-sequenced VSAM file is to be accessed
using only a primary key. Sometimes, though, you may want to use
other fields to access the records in a file. You can do this by coding
additional functions in the DEFINE CLUSTER command. Because the
use of alternate keys is beyond the scope of this book, I'm not going to
cover it. I just want you to be aware of it, since you may run into it in
your shop.

The DEFINE CLUSTER statement is also used to assign
passwords to VSAM clusters. VSAM uses a complicated password
protection structure, so I'm not going to show you how to assign
passwords here. If you need to assign passwords, you can find out
how in the IBM manual.

DISCUSSION

At this point, you may be thinking that a lot of unnecessary effort is
required just to establish a VSAM file. However, the extra effort
made to create the file is justified by the fact that VSAM files are
easy to process once they've been created. For example, to retrieve a

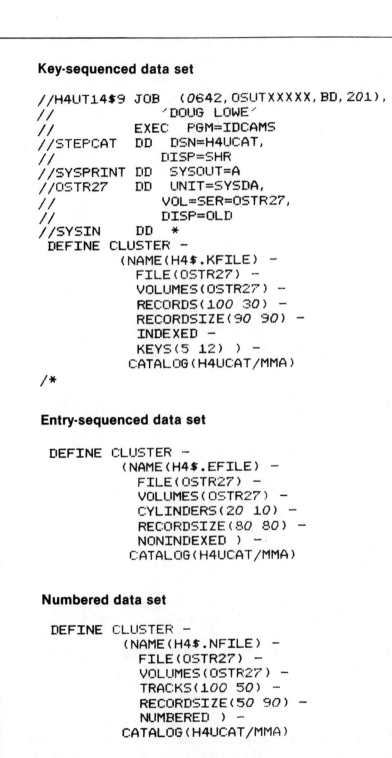

```
Key-sequenced data set

//H4UT14$9 JOB   (0642,OSUTXXXXX,BD,201),
//             'DOUG LOWE'
//          EXEC  PGM=IDCAMS
//STEPCAT   DD   DSN=H4UCAT,
//             DISP=SHR
//SYSPRINT DD   SYSOUT=A
//OSTR27    DD   UNIT=SYSDA,
//             VOL=SER=OSTR27,
//             DISP=OLD
//SYSIN     DD  *
 DEFINE CLUSTER -
         (NAME(H4$.KFILE) -
          FILE(OSTR27) -
          VOLUMES(OSTR27) -
          RECORDS(100 30) -
          RECORDSIZE(90 90) -
          INDEXED -
          KEYS(5 12) ) -
         CATALOG(H4UCAT/MMA)
/*


Entry-sequenced data set

 DEFINE CLUSTER -
         (NAME(H4$.EFILE) -
          FILE(OSTR27) -
          VOLUMES(OSTR27) -
          CYLINDERS(20 10) -
          RECORDSIZE(80 80) -
          NONINDEXED ) -
         CATALOG(H4UCAT/MMA)


Numbered data set

 DEFINE CLUSTER -
         (NAME(H4$.NFILE) -
          FILE(OSTR27) -
          VOLUMES(OSTR27) -
          TRACKS(100 50) -
          RECORDSIZE(50 90) -
          NUMBERED ) -
         CATALOG(H4UCAT/MMA)
```

Figure 14-9   Creating VSAM data set clusters using IDCAMS

VSAM data set, you only need to specify DSN and DISP in the DD statement. And VSAM automatically takes care of space allocation, so you don't have to worry about using up the space originally allocated. Furthermore, VSAM automatically reorganizes VSAM files so they are as efficient as possible. In short, it is well worth the effort required to create VSAM files.

Terminology

user catalog

master catalog

data space

cluster

Objective

Given a problem involving the definition of a VSAM area, code the appropriate JCL and control statements for its solution.

3   # TOPIC 3   Copying and Printing with IDCAMS

Two common utility functions performed by IDCAMS are copying and printing files. IDCAMS can copy or print VSAM or non-VSAM files. For copy operations, the REPRO statement is used; for print operations, the PRINT statement is used. In this topic, I'll show you how to use both statements.

COPYING FILES WITH IDCAMS

Figure 14-10 illustrates the REPRO statement, used for copy operations. As you can see, REPRO uses only two parameters. INFILE specifies a DD statement that defines the input file, and OUTFILE specifies a DD statement that defines the output file. If the file is password protected, the password must be specified in the INFILE and OUTFILE parameters.

The input file may be any type of VSAM file (key-sequenced, entry-sequenced, or numbered) or a non-VSAM sequential or ISAM file. The output file may be any type of VSAM file or a sequential non-VSAM file. ISAM files are not allowed for output. The REPRO statement doesn't indicate the file type. Instead, the file type is

---

The REPRO statement

```
REPRO  INFILE(ddname/password) -
       OUTFILE(ddname/password)
```

Explanation

INFILE   Identifies the input file's DD statement and password.

OUTFILE   Identifies the output file's DD statement and password.

Figure 14-10   The REPRO statement

specified by the DEFINE command that defined the cluster (for VSAM files) or the JCL (for non-VSAM files).

Figure 14-11 shows a job that copies a VSAM file named H4$.INVTRAN. The output is another VSAM file named H4$.ITRAN2. Since the output file is a VSAM file, it must have been defined previously with a DEFINE statement. That's why the ITRAN2 DD statement specifies DISP = OLD.

Figure 14-12 shows an IDCAMS job that loads a VSAM file from a non-VSAM file. Here, the input file is defined in the JCL as H4.INVTRAN, and the output file is a VSAM file named H4$.INVTRAN. I didn't specify whether the VSAM file is an entry-sequenced, key-sequenced, or numbered file because that information is stored in the catalog. It's possible to load a key-sequenced file from a sequential file—IDCAMS simply determines the proper key based on the information supplied when the file was defined. IDCAMS can also accept an ISAM file as input and generate a key-sequenced, entry-sequenced, or numbered file as output.

Figure 14-13 shows a job that copies a VSAM file to a non-VSAM file. Here, the JCL defines the input file as a VSAM file named H4$.INVTRAN, and the output file as a new sequential file named H4.ITRAN.BACKUP. Remember that a non-VSAM output file must be sequential—ISAM is not allowed.

I hope you can see the flexibility of the IDCAMS copy function from these examples. You can copy VSAM and non-VSAM files in any combination as long as the output file isn't ISAM. One limitation you should recognize, though, is that unlike the IEBGENER utility, IDCAMS doesn't allow you to rearrange the individual fields in the data records. If you need to change the format of a VSAM record, you have to copy the file to a sequential, non-VSAM file, edit the records with IEBGENER, and then reload the file with IDCAMS.

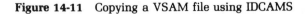

```
//H4UT1411 JOB   (0642,QSUTXXXXX,BD,201),
//                'DOUG LOWE'
//          EXEC  PGM=IDCAMS
//SYSPRINT DD   SYSOUT=A
//INVTRAN  DD   DSN=H4$.INVTRAN,
//              DISP=OLD
//ITRAN2   DD   DSN=H4$.ITRAN2,
//              DISP=OLD
//SYSIN    DD  *
 REPRO INFILE(INVTRAN) -
       OUTFILE(ITRAN2)
/*
```

Figure 14-11   Copying a VSAM file using IDCAMS

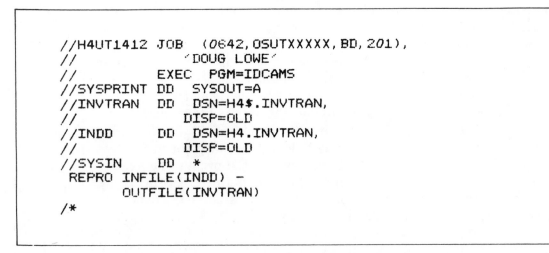

```
//H4UT1412 JOB   (0642,QSUTXXXXX,BD,201),
//                'DOUG LOWE'
//          EXEC  PGM=IDCAMS
//SYSPRINT DD   SYSOUT=A
//INVTRAN  DD   DSN=H4$.INVTRAN,
//              DISP=OLD
//INDD     DD   DSN=H4.INVTRAN,
//              DISP=OLD
//SYSIN    DD  *
 REPRO INFILE(INDD) -
       OUTFILE(INVTRAN)
/*
```

Figure 14-12   Loading a VSAM file from a non-VSAM file using IDCAMS

PRINTING FILES

The PRINT statement, shown in figure 14-14, is used for all IDCAMS printing operations. As you can see, its format is simple. INFILE specifies the ddname and password (if required) of the input file. Coding CHARACTER, HEX, or DUMP specifies the format of the printed output. (DUMP is the default if no format is coded.) If CHARACTER is specified, the output is printed exactly as it appears in the input record. If HEX is specified, each character is converted to a two-character hexadecimal code before printing. If DUMP is coded, the output is printed in both forms, much like a storage dump.

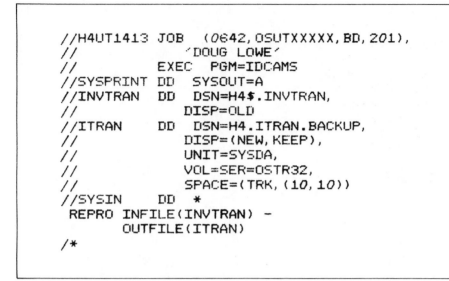

```
//H4UT1413 JOB   (0642,OSUTXXXXX,BD,201),
//               'DOUG LOWE'
//          EXEC  PGM=IDCAMS
//SYSPRINT DD  SYSOUT=A
//INVTRAN  DD  DSN=H4$.INVTRAN,
//               DISP=OLD
//ITRAN    DD  DSN=H4.ITRAN.BACKUP,
//               DISP=(NEW,KEEP),
//               UNIT=SYSDA,
//               VOL=SER=OSTR32,
//               SPACE=(TRK,(10,10))
//SYSIN    DD  *
 REPRO INFILE(INVTRAN) -
       OUTFILE(ITRAN)
/*
```

Figure 14-13   Copying a VSAM file to a non-VSAM file using IDCAMS

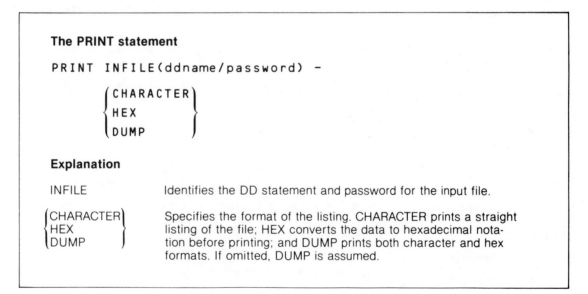

The PRINT statement

```
PRINT INFILE(ddname/password) -

      {CHARACTER}
      {HEX      }
      {DUMP     }
```

Explanation

INFILE	Identifies the DD statement and password for the input file.
{CHARACTER} {HEX} {DUMP}	Specifies the format of the listing. CHARACTER prints a straight listing of the file; HEX converts the data to hexadecimal notation before printing; and DUMP prints both character and hex formats. If omitted, DUMP is assumed.

Figure 14-14   The PRINT statement

To illustrate the use of the PRINT statement, consider figure 14-15. Although a VSAM file is printed in this example, a non-VSAM file (sequential or ISAM) can be printed by IDCAMS as well. The bottom part of this figure shows how the output appears for an entry-sequenced file. The format used for key-sequenced and numbered files is the same except for the way the records are numbered. (For entry-sequenced files, IDCAMS prints the relative byte address, or

The JCL

```
//H4UT1415 JOB   (0642,OSUTXXXXX,BD,201),
//              'DOUG LOWE'
//         EXEC  PGM=IDCAMS
//SYSPRINT DD   SYSOUT=A
//INVTRAN  DD   DSN=H4$.INVTRAN,
//              DISP=OLD
//SYSIN    DD   *
 PRINT INFILE(INVTRAN) -
         CHARACTER
/*
```

Resulting output

```
IDCAMS   SYSTEM SERVICES


LISTING OF DATA SET -H4$.INVTRAN

RBA OF RECORD - 0
01203102350002564002645601564000015640000001654015205610540001601540

RBA OF RECORD - 80
01687900890040400006510000546054600440000456400010654000010005460001

RBA OF RECORD - 160
00564000490156054003249805684001980048940089700098700654456000054500

RBA OF RECORD - 240
05407894560000000000013546871510000156154100000000000000000000000000

RBA OF RECORD - 320
16874400267480026500259820000154001240078900126400018900155670004898

RBA OF RECORD - 400
02211022004470014700156002580013500154001230054600123005480013540012
.
.
.
RBA OF RECORD - 2048
02222022004470024700156002580013500154001230054600123005480013540012

RBA OF RECORD - 2128
05877702540252045805620325698502475025632025874202589632025820000000

IDC0005I NUMBER OF RECORDS PROCESSED WAS 26

IDC0001I FUNCTION COMPLETED, HIGHEST CONDITION CODE WAS 0
```

Figure 14-15 Printing a VSAM file in CHARACTER format using IDCAMS

RBA, of each record; for key-sequenced files, the record key is printed; and for numbered files, the relative record number is printed.

Figure 14-16 is a listing of the same file produced with the DUMP option. Here, the left-hand side of the listing gives a hexadecimal listing of the data. On the right, the data is printed in character format. Because this format takes more room than the CHARACTER format, I recommend you don't use it unless you must.

DISCUSSION

Since the REPRO and PRINT statements are so easy to use, I have only covered them briefly here. With the information and examples contained in this topic, you should have no trouble using IDCAMS to copy or print VSAM or non-VSAM files. Although you may code additional options on the REPRO and PRINT statements, they aren't used very often.

Objective

Given a problem that involves copying or printing a VSAM or non-VSAM file, code an IDCAMS job for its solution.

```
IDCAMS  SYSTEM SERVICES

LISTING OF DATA SET -H4$.INVTRAN

RBA OF RECORD - 0
0000  F0F1F2F0 F3F1F0F2 F3F5F0F0 F0F2F5F6   F4F0F0F2 F6F4F5F6 F0F1F5F6 F4F0F0F0   *0120310235000256400264560156400*
0020  F0F1F5F6 F4F0F0F0 F0F0F0F1 F6F5F4F0   F1F5F2F0 F5F4F0F0 F0F1F6F0             *0456500000165401520561054000160*
0040  F1F5F4F0 40404040 40404040                                                   *1540                           *

RBA OF RECORD - 80
0000  F0F1F6F8 F7F9F0F0 F8F9F0F0 F4F0F0F0   F0F0F0F6 F5F1F0F0 F0F1F5F4 F6F0F0F5F4   *0168790089004040000651000546054*
0020  F6F0F0F0 F4F4F5F6 F4F0F0F0 40404040   F1F0F6F5 F4F0F0F0 F0F1F0F0             *6004400045640001065400001000546*
0040  F0F0F0F1 40404040 40404040                                                   *0001                           *

RBA OF RECORD - 160
0000  F0F0F5F6 F4F0F0F0 F4F9F0F1 F5F6F0F5   F4F0F0F3 F2F4F9F8 F0F5F6F0F8 F4F0F0F1  *0056400049015605400324980568400 1*
0020  F9F8F0F0 F4F8F9F4 F0F0F8F9 F7F0F0F0   F9F8F7F0 F0F6F5F4 F4F5F6F0             *98004894008970009870065445600005*
0040  F4F5F0F0 40404040 40404040                                                   *4500                           *

RBA OF RECORD - 240
0000  F0F5F4F0 F7F8F9F4 F5F6F0F0 F0F0F0F0   F0F0F0F0 F0F1F3F5 F4F6F8F7 F1F5F1F0    *0540789456000000000001354687151 0*
0020  F0F0F0F1 F5F6F1F5 F4F1F0F0 F0F0F0F0   F0F0F0F0 F0F0F0F0 F0F0F0F0             *0001561541000000000000000000000*
0040  F0F0F0F0 40404040 40404040                                                   *0000                           *

. . .

RBA OF RECORD - 2048
0000  F0F2F2F2 F2F0F2F2 F0F0F4F4 F7F0F0F2   F4F4F7F0F0 F1F5F6F0 F0F2F5F8 F0F0F1F3  *0222220220447001560025800013*
0020  F5F0F0F0 F1F2F3F0 F0F0F4F4 40404040   F0F0F0F1F2 F3F0F0F5 F4F8F0F0 F1F3F5F4  *5001540012300548001354*
0040  F0F0F1F2 40404040 40404040                                                   *0012                           *

RBA OF RECORD - 2128
0000  F0F5F8F7 F7F7F0F2 F5F4F0F0 F5F2F0F4   F5F5F8F0F5 F6F2F0F3 F2F5F6F9 F8F5F0F2  *0587770254025204580562032569850 2*
0020  F4F7F5F0 F2F5F6F3 F2F0F0F4 40404040   F0F2F5F8F8 F9F6F3F2 F0F2F5F8 F2F0F0F0  *47502563202587420258963202582000*
0040  F0F0F0F0 40404040 40404040                                                   *0000                           *

IDC0005I NUMBER OF RECORDS PROCESSED WAS 26

IDC0001I FUNCTION COMPLETED, HIGHEST CONDITION CODE WAS 0
```

Figure 14-16 Printout of a VSAM file in DUMP format using IDCAMS

TOPIC 4   IDCAMS Catalog Maintenance Functions

In this topic, I'm going to show you how to use a few of the IDCAMS catalog maintenance functions. The functions correspond to the non-VSAM catalog maintenance functions performed by IEHPROGM and IEHLIST. First, I'm going to show you how to use the LISTCAT statement to list the contents of a VSAM catalog. Then, I'll show you how to perform various catalog maintenance functions such as deleting files, renaming files, and cataloging non-VSAM files.

LISTING A VSAM CATALOG

Figure 14-17 shows the format of the LISTCAT statement, which is used to list the contents of a VSAM catalog. As you can see, you may code several parameters. The first, CATALOG, specifies the name of the catalog to be listed. If CATALOG is omitted, the master catalog or the JOBCAT or STEPCAT override catalog is listed.

The next two parameters, ENTRIES and type, are used to specify that only certain catalog entries are to be listed. If ENTRIES is coded, it specifies the names of the catalog entries to be listed. If type is coded, it specifies that only certain types of catalog entries are to be listed (such as clusters, non-VSAM, indexed, etc.). If no type is specified, all entries are listed.

The last parameter specifies the information that is to be printed for each entry. If you specify NAME, only the name and entry type of each entry is listed. If you specify VOLUME, IDCAMS lists the name, entry type, owner-id, creation and expiration dates, and the volume containing the file. You may code many other values here as well, but NAME and VOLUME are the most useful.

Figure 14-18 shows a job that lists the contents of a VSAM catalog. Here, all of the cluster entries in the catalog are listed with the NAME format. The bottom part of the figure shows the output generated by this job. As you can see, the listing isn't very easy to read. For each VSAM data set, the listing shows the cluster name and the name of the elements containing the data and index. In addition, the listing shows the catalog containing the entry for each element (SYSV.VSAMC1 for each element listed in figure 14-18).

CATALOG MAINTENANCE

VSAM catalog maintenance is performed by IDCAMS using three statements: DELETE, ALTER, and DEFINE NONVSAM. These are illustrated in figure 14-19. The DELETE statement is used primarily to

---

The LISTCAT statement

```
LISTCAT CATALOG(catalog-name/password) -
        ENTRIES(name/password,...) -
        type -
       ⎧NAME  ⎫
       ⎨VOLUME⎬
       ⎩ALL   ⎭
```

Explanation

CATALOG
: Specifies the name and password of the catalog to be listed. If omitted, the master catalog or the catalog specified in a JOBCAT or STEPCAT statement is used.

ENTRIES
: Specifies the names and passwords of entries to be listed. If omitted, all entries are listed.

type
: Specifies the type of entries to be listed. If omitted, all types of entries are listed. Possible values are: CLUSTER, DATA, INDEX, NONVSAM, and SPACE. (See the IBM manual for other values.)

⎧NAME⎫
⎨VOLUME⎬
⎩ALL⎭
: Specifies what information is to be listed. NAME lists the name and type of each entry. VOLUME lists the name, entry type, owner-id, creation and expiration dates, and the volume containing the file. ALL lists all the fields for each entry. (See the IBM manual for other values that may be coded here.)

Figure 14-17   The LISTCAT statement

remove entries from a VSAM catalog. The ALTER statement is used to change entries. DEFINE NONVSAM is used to enter non-VSAM files into the VSAM catalog.

Figure 14-20 shows an IDCAMS job that uses the DELETE statement to delete several catalog entries. The first DELETE statement simply specifies that all entries made under the name H4$.ITRAN2 should be deleted. The second DELETE statement says to delete only the cluster entry for a file named H4$.TRCMS. The last DELETE statement tells IDCAMS to remove the entry for a non-VSAM file named H4.ARMAST from the VSAM catalog. The SCRATCH parameter simply says to remove the H4.ARMAST entry from the VTOC as well. If SCRATCH isn't coded, the non-VSAM file would simply be uncataloged.

Figure 14-21 shows how the ALTER command can be used to change the name of a VSAM data set. Here, the first parameter

The JCL

```
//H4UT1418 JOB   (0642,OSUTXXXXX,BD,201),
//              'DOUG LOWE'
//          EXEC   PGM=IDCAMS
//SYSPRINT DD   SYSOUT=A
//SYSIN    DD   *
 LISTCAT CLUSTER -
         NAME
/*
```

Resulting output

```
 IDCAMS   SYSTEM SERVICES

  LISTCAT CLUSTER -
          NAME
 CLUSTER ------- H4$.ARTRANS
      IN-CAT --- SYSV.VSAMC1
      DATA ------- VSAMDSET.T9623CA0.DFD80304.T90FE2C2.T9623CA0
      IN-CAT --- SYSV.VSAMC1
 CLUSTER ------- H4$.EOSMAS
      IN-CAT --- SYSV.VSAMC1
      DATA ------- VSAMDSET.TD61F310.DFD80304.T90FE2C3.TD61F310
      IN-CAT --- SYSV.VSAMC1
 CLUSTER ------- H4$.ITRAN2
      IN-CAT --- SYSV.VSAMC1
      DATA ------- VSAMDSET.TD428050.DFD80304.T90FE2BA.TD428050
      IN-CAT --- SYSV.VSAMC1
 CLUSTER ------- H4$.ARMAST
      IN-CAT --- SYSV.VSAMC1
      DATA ------- VSAMDSET.T5119310.DFD80304.T90FE2BC.T5119310
      IN-CAT --- SYSV.VSAMC1
      INDEX ------- VSAMDSET.T5119790.DFD80304.T90FE2BC.T5119790
      IN-CAT --- SYSV.VSAMC1
 CLUSTER ------- H4$.TJKKMST
      IN-CAT --- SYSV.VSAMC1
      DATA ------- VSAMDSET.TACED1A0.DFD80304.T90FE2C0.TACED1A0
      IN-CAT --- SYSV.VSAMC1
      INDEX ------- VSAMDSET.TACED630.DFD80304.T90FE2C0.TACED630
      IN-CAT --- SYSV.VSAMC1
```

Figure 14-18   Listing a VSAM catalog using IDCAMS

specifies the old name of the file (H4$.INVTRAN), and the NEWNAME parameter specifies the new file name (H4$.ICTRAN). Although the ALTER command has dozens of subparameters, it would be beyond the scope of this book to cover them here. So if you need to change any item in a catalog entry other than the entry name, consult the IBM manual to determine the correct parameter.

The DELETE statement

```
DELETE (entry-name/password,...) -
        type -
        SCRATCH -
        CATALOG(catalog-name/password)
```

Explanation

entry — name   Specifies the names of the entries to be deleted.

type   Specifies the type of entries to be deleted. Possible values are CLUSTER, SPACE, NONVSAM. (See the IBM manual for other values.)

SCRATCH   Indicates that a NONVSAM file should be scratched from the VTOC as well as from the VSAM catalog.

CATALOG   Specifies the name and password of the catalog containing the file.

The ALTER statement

```
ALTER (entry-name/password) -
        NEWNAME(newname)
```

Explanation

entry — name   Specifies the name of the entry to be altered.

NEWNAME   Specifies a new name for the entry.

Note: There are many other options for the ALTER statement, but NEWNAME is the most commonly used.

Figure 14-19   IDCAMS catalog maintenance statements (part 1 of 2)

Figure 14-22 shows how the DEFINE NONVSAM command is used to enter a non-VSAM file into a VSAM catalog. Here, the file name is H4.BJTRAN, the device type is SYSDA, and the volume name is OSTR32. Once a non-VSAM file is entered into a VSAM catalog, you only need to specify DSNAME and DISP to access it.

DISCUSSION

This has of course been a brief discussion of the catalog maintenance functions available with IDCAMS. I have only covered the basic func-

The DEFINE NONVSAM statement

```
DEFINE NONVSAM
         (NAME(entry-name) -
          DEVICETYPES(device-types) -
          VOLUMES(vol-ser) -
          OWNER(owner-id) ) -
       CATALOG(catalog-name/password)
```

Explanation

NAME	Specifies the data set name of the non-VSAM file to be cataloged.
DEVICETYPES	Specifies the device type (UNIT) of the file.
VOLUMES	Specifies the volume serial number of the volume containing the file.
OWNER	Specifies the owner name.
CATALOG	Specifies the name and password of the catalog that will contain the entry If omitted, the STEPCAT, JOBCAT, or master catalog will be used.

Figure 14-19   IDCAMS catalog maintenance statements (part 2 of 2)

tions you are likely to require. If you need to do more advanced catalog maintenance functions, consult the IBM manuals. One other point: whenever you are performing catalog maintenance functions, be sure to follow the standards established by your installation. If, for example, your installation has a rule against cataloging non-VSAM files in a user catalog, don't do it.

Objective

Given a problem involving VSAM catalog maintenance, code an acceptable IDCAMS job for its solution.

```
//H4UT1420 JOB   (0642,OSUTXXXXX,BD,201),
//             ´DOUG LOWE´
//        EXEC  PGM=IDCAMS
//SYSPRINT DD   SYSOUT=A
//SYSIN     DD  *
 DELETE (H4$.ITRAN2/MMA)
 DELETE (H4$.TRCMS/MMA) -
         CLUSTER
 DELETE (H4.ARMAST/MMA) -
         SCRATCH
/*
```

Figure 14-20 Deleting VSAM catalog entries using IDCAMS

```
//H4UT1421 JOB   (0642,OSUTXXXXX,BD,201),
//             ´DOUG LOWE´
//        EXEC  PGM=IDCAMS
//SYSPRINT DD   SYSOUT=A
//SYSIN     DD  *
 ALTER (H4$.INVTRAN/MMA) -
        NEWNAME(H4$.ICTRAN)
/*
```

Figure 14-21 Renaming a VSAM file using IDCAMS

```
//H4UT1422 JOB   (0642,OSUTXXXXX,BD,201),
//             ´DOUG LOWE´
//        EXEC  PGM=IDCAMS
//SYSPRINT DD   SYSOUT=A
//SYSIN     DD  *
 DEFINE NONVSAM -
        (NAME(H4.BJTRAN) -
         DEVICETYPES(SYSDA) -
         VOLUMES(OSTR32) )
/*
```

Figure 14-22 Cataloging a non-VSAM file in a VSAM catalog using IDCAMS

Field Name	Transact Code
racteristics	X
Usage	
Position	1

rvice le-1	Service Charge-1	Se Cos
3)	9(5)V99	9(5

Appendix A

Utility Functions

Function	Utility	Page
Create:		
an empty data set	IEFBR14	130
ISAM test data	IEBDG	83
a partitioned data set	IEBUPDTE	66
sequential test data	IEBDG	80
Define:		
a VSAM catalog	IDCAMS	155
a VSAM cluster	IDCAMS	157
a VSAM data space	IDCAMS	157
Delete:		
a data set	IEHPROGM	124
	IEFBR14	130
a member of a partitioned data set	IEHPROGM	121
a non-VSAM file in a VSAM catalog	IDCAMS	167
a VSAM file	IDCAMS	167
Edit:		
records in a partitioned member	IEBUPDTE	69
records in a sequential file	IEBGENER	16
List:		
a partitioned data set directory	IEHLIST	99
entries in a system catalog	IEHLIST	104
entries in a VSAM catalog	IDCAMS	167
entries in a VTOC	IEHLIST	101
Load:		
an ISAM file from an unloaded file	IEBISAM	42
an ISAM file from sequential input	IEBDG	83
a VSAM file from a non-VSAM file	IDCAMS	161
Merge:		
partitioned data sets	IEBCOPY	52
sequential files	SORT/MERGE	144
Move:		
a member of a partitioned data set	IEHMOVE	115
a partitioned data set	IEHMOVE	113
a sequential file	IEHMOVE	113

Function	Utility	Page
Print:		
an ISAM file	IEBISAM	43
a member of a partitioned data set	IEBPTPCH	34
a non-VSAM file	IDCAMS	162
a sequential file	IEBGENER	15
	IEBPTPCH	30
a VSAM file	IDCAMS	162
Punch:		
a member of a partitioned data set	IEBPTPCH	34
a sequential file	IEBPTPCH	34
Reorganize records in a sequential file	IEBGENER	16
Scratch:		
a data set	IEHPROGM	124
	IEFBR14	131
a member of a partitioned data set	IEHPROGM	121
a non-VSAM file in a VSAM catalog	IDCAMS	167
a VSAM file	IDCAMS	167
Sort the records in a sequential file	SORT/MERGE	144
Uncatalog a data set	IEHPROGM	124
	IEFBR14	131
Unload:		
an ISAM file	IEBISAM	42
a partitioned data set	IEHMOVE	113

```
080114 MIF 02247000011
080A88 MIN 02000000008
080666 RTM 08920000040
080447
080661
080551 MIN 00200000000
080551
080773 XIM 00075000003
080118 ABC 00100000000
080225 AFS 00300000001
080886 MIN 01000000005
080447
080774 ABC 06000000040
080666
080118 GHI 00300000001
080882 MIS 00052000000
```

Appendix B

Return Codes

All of the utility programs return a condition code indicating the results of the utility's execution. A return code of zero always indicates that the utility executed successfully. Other codes, such as 4, 8, 12, or 16, indicate possible error conditions that the utility encountered. This appendix presents a table showing the meaning of the return codes produced by the utilities covered in this book.

In the table, an expression like *recoverable error* means that the utility encountered an error that did not cause it to stop processing. Usually, the results will be inaccurate when a recoverable error is encountered. *Terminated because of error condition* means that the utility was unable to continue execution due to an error. *Terminated by user routine* means that a user routine returned a control code indicating that the utility should terminate. The other reasons given in the table should be self-explanatory.

Return Code

Utility	0	4	8	12	16
IEBGENER	Successful completion	Recoverable error	Recoverable error	Terminated because of error	Terminated by user routine
IEBPTPCH	Successful completion	Empty data set	Member not found	Terminated because of error	Terminated by user routine
IEBISAM	Successful completion	Terminated by user routine	Terminated because of error	Terminated by user routine	Terminated because of error
IEBCOPY	Successful completion	Recoverable error	Terminated because of error	—	—
IEBUPDTE	Successful completion	Control statement error	—	Terminated because of error	Terminated by user routine
IEBDG	Successful completion	Terminated by user routine	Control statement error	Terminated because of error	Terminated because of error

Return Code

Utility	0	4	8	12	16
IEBCOMPR	Successful completion	—	Unequal comparison	Terminated because of error	Terminated by user routine
IEHLIST	Successful completion	—	Recoverable error	Terminated because of error	Terminated because of error
IEHMOVE	Successful completion	Recoverable error	Recoverable error	Terminated because of error	—
IEHPROGM	Successful completion	Control statement error	Recoverable error	Terminated because of error	Terminated because of error
Sort/Merge	Successful completion	—	—	—	Unsuccessful completion
IDCAMS	Successful completion	Warning message issued	Recoverable error	Recoverable error	Terminated because of error

Index

Order Form

Our Unlimited Guarantee

To our customers who order directly from us: You must be satisfied. Our books must work for you, or you can send them back for a full refund . . . no matter how many you buy, no matter how long you've had them.

Name & Title _____

Company (if company address) _____

Address_____

City, State, Zip _____

Phone number (including area code) _____

Qty	Product code and title	Price

OS Subjects

Qty	Code	Title	Price
_____	MJCL	MVS JCL	$32.50
_____	TSO	MVS TSO	25.00
_____	OSUT	OS Utilities	15.00
_____	OSDB	OS Debugging for the COBOL Programmer	20.00

Assembler Language

Qty	Code	Title	Price
_____	MBAL	MVS Assembler Language	$30.00
_____	VBAL	DOS/VSE Assembler Language	30.00

DOS/VSE Subjects

Qty	Code	Title	Price
_____	VJCL	DOS/VSE JCL	$30.00
_____	ICCF	DOS/VSE ICCF	25.00

VM/CMS

Qty	Code	Title	Price
_____	VMCC	VM/CMS: Commands and Concepts	$25.00

COBOL Language Elements

Qty	Code	Title	Price
_____	SC1R	Structured ANS COBOL: Part 1	$25.00
_____	SC2R	Structured ANS COBOL: Part 2	25.00
_____	RW	Report Writer	13.50

VSAM

Qty	Code	Title	Price
_____	VSMX	VSAM: Access Method Services and Application Programming	$25.00
_____	VSAM	VSAM for the COBOL Programmer	15.00

CICS

Qty	Code	Title	Price
_____	CIC1	CICS for the COBOL Programmer: Part 1	$25.00
_____	CIC2	CICS for the COBOL Programmer: Part 2	25.00
_____	CREF	The CICS Programmer's Desk Reference	32.50

Data Base Processing

Qty	Code	Title	Price
_____	IMS1	IMS for the COBOL Programmer Part 1: DL/I Data Base Processing	$30.00
_____	IMS2	IMS for the COBOL Programmer Part 2: Data Communications and MFS	30.00

System Development

Qty	Code	Title	Price
_____	DDBS	How to Design and Develop Business Systems	$20.00

☐ Bill me the appropriate price plus UPS shipping and handling (and sales tax in California) for each book ordered.

☐ Bill the appropriate book prices plus UPS shipping and handling (and sales tax in California) to my _____ VISA _____ MasterCard:

Card number _____
Valid thru (month/year)_____
Cardowner's signature_____
(not valid without signature)

☐ I want to **save** UPS shipping and handling charges. Here's my check or money order for $_____. California residents, please add 6% sales tax to your total. (Offer valid in the U.S. only.)

To order more quickly,

Call **toll-free** 1-800-221-5528

(Weekdays, 9 to 4 Pacific Std. Time)

In California, call 1-800-221-5527

Mike Murach & Associates, Inc.

4697 West Jacquelyn Avenue
Fresno, California 93722
(209) 275-3335

Comment Form

Your opinions count

If you have comments, criticisms, or suggestions, I'm eager to get them. Your opinions today will effect our products of tomorrow. If you have questions, you can expect an answer within one week from the time we receive them. And if you discover any errors in this product, typographical or otherwise, please point them out so we can make corrections when the product is reprinted.

Thanks for your help.

Mike Murach
Fresno, California

fold   fold

Book title: OS Utilities

Dear Mike: _____

_____

_____

_____

_____

_____

_____

_____

_____

fold _____ fold

_____

_____

Name and Title_____

Company (if any)_____

Address_____

City, State, & Zip_____

Fold where indicated and seal.
No postage necessary if mailed in the United States.